new vegetarian

celia brooks brown

photography by philip webb

new vegetarian

bold and beautiful recipes for every occasion

RYLAND
PETERS
& SMALL

LONDON NEW YORK

Senior Designer	Paul Tilby
Commissioning Editor	Elsa Petersen-Schepelern
Editor	Maddalena Bastianelli
Production	Meryl Silbert
Art Director	Gabriella Le Grazie
Publishing Director	Alison Starling
Food Stylist	Celia Brooks Brown
Food Stylist's Assistant	Kate Habershon
Stylist	Malena Burgess
Indexer	Hilary Bird

First published in Great Britain in 2001
by Ryland Peters & Small
20–21 Jockey's Fields, London WC1R 4BW
www.rylandpeters.com

This paperback edition first published in 2005

10 9 8 7 6 5 4 3 2 1

ISBN 1 84172 983 3

A catalogue record for this book is available from
the British Library.

Printed in China.

NOTES

All spoon measurements are level unless
otherwise stated.

All fruits and vegetables should be washed
thoroughly and peeled, unless otherwise
stated. Unwaxed citrus fruits should be used
whenever possible.

Barbecues, ovens and grills should be heated
to the required temperature – if using a fan-
assisted oven, cooking times should be reduced
according to the manufacturer's instructions.

Specialist Asian ingredients are available in large
supermarkets, Thai and Chinese shops,
as well as Asian stores.

for Mom

AUTHOR ACKNOWLEDGEMENTS

I am deeply grateful to Eric Treuille and the team at Books for Cooks for their
infinite support and encouragement. Huge thanks to Elsa and Maddie for their hard
work and stoic patience. Much heartfelt gratitude to Philip Webb for creating such
vivacious pictures, and to Kate Habershon, Lizzie Harris, Paul Tilby and Sarah Cuttle
for making the photo shoot such brilliant fun. I extend warm appreciation to all
who participated in my home tastings (and endured a cold, dark barbecue in
February) – Fisher, Ben, Callum, Alex, Sarah, Jessica, James, Sarah W., Tarda,
Mark J., Dom, Julia, Paula, Paulie and Steve M.– and to my gorgeous husband Dan
for telling it like it is.

Thanks also to Michael van Straten for nutritional advice, and The Vegetarian
Society (www.vegsoc.org) for invaluable information.

contents

introduction

Welcome to the new era of vegetarian cooking and eating! It's food for a dynamic life through a healthy diet – and food for the sheer enjoyment of it. It's food modelled on ancient world cuisines, as well as fusing the myriad of modern ingredients available to us today.

Every day, more people are deciding to eat less meat or are giving it up altogether. Cooking vegetarian can require a little more creativity than cooking with meat, but that doesn't mean it has to be complicated. This book aims to inspire both the seasoned cook and the novice, too.

New vegetarian cooking and eating is not about finding substitutes for meat, but rather about shifting the focus. Instead of the conventional 'meat and two veg', meals without meat should be a varied composition of texture, colour and flavour. Imagine a plate of mezze – creamy hoummus singing with garlic, olives twinkling like jewels, smoky grilled vegetables and grains dressed in fresh lemon juice and peppery olive oil – and a warm and soft pocket of pillowy flatbread to scoop it all up. Do you miss the meat?

BEING VEGETARIAN

There are many reasons for being vegetarian and even if you aren't one, you probably know someone who is. Some of the most common reasons for being vegetarian or cutting down on meat are:

- You may want a healthy diet to give you a greater sense of well-being.

- You may boycott meat because you don't agree with the animal husbandry methods used in the meat and poultry industries.
- You may have environmental concerns.
- You may have religious reasons.
- You may, like me, have a natural dislike for, or indifference towards meat.

Whatever the reason, the health benefits are clear. The World Health Organization recommends a diet that is low in saturated animal fats and high in complex carbohydrates, as found in fruits, vegetables, grains and pulses – typical of many vegetarian diets. Organizations such as the British Medical Association claim that vegetarians may be less likely to develop heart disease, high blood pressure, certain forms of cancer and many other health problems.

All the reasons for living without meat are good ones. Just remember, no one likes a preaching vegetarian. Celebrate being a vegetarian for the positive reasons, and enjoy a life of cooking and eating truly good food.

BUY FRESH, SEASONAL AND, IF POSSIBLE, ORGANIC

The fruits of the earth are the main elements of vegetarian eating. Everyone has a built-in self-defence mechanism which makes us sensitive to food that might be harmful to us – it smells odd, looks discoloured, lacks lustre. But foods can deceive us – a bag of perky supermarket salad may look fresh, but why? Why are winter greenhouse tomatoes tasteless bullets? Fresh produce is delicate, so it is usually treated – with preservatives, wax, gas or irradiation – to sustain its long journey to the supermarket shelves. By purchasing food in season and from as local a source as possible – such as farmers' markets – you'll get fresher, purer produce. The impact on the environment will be less too, as thousands of gallons of airline fuel and diesel go into transporting out-of-season produce across vast distances.

The use of toxic pesticides and artificial fertilizers in the intensive farming of crops does increase productivity, and has shaped the evolution of modern agriculture – but this has had unfortunate consequences. Quality and flavour are compromised by rapid production, toxic residues end up in our food and the environment becomes polluted. The only way to be absolutely certain that your food is safe and additive-free is to buy certified organic ingredients. It means spending a little more money, but it's worth it for flavour, health and peace of mind.

The issue of genetically modified or GM foods is another concern. Genetic modification involves the insertion of a gene from one species into another. The aim is to make life easier for the producer, but what about the consumer? It is not yet known what the long-term effects of consuming GM foods will be, nor what effect GM will have on the environment. A soybean plant engineered to resist herbicide can then be sprayed liberally with toxic, non-biodegradable chemicals that end up in the food chain – and ultimately on our plates. Buying organic is one way to avoid GM products, and even then there's some risk.

RELAX AND ENJOY!

Remember, ultimately food is fun. If you can spend time shopping and sourcing the best ingredients, it can be hugely rewarding, especially when you come to eat it.

Whenever we get stressed or worried about cooking, it never seems to taste as good. But don't think of cooking as a chore – it can be very relaxing. Read the recipe carefully and, if you think you can make it, try it. As your confidence grows, you'll find that the satisfaction in the end result is much greater than the effort you put in. Eventually you will want to play around with the recipes and add your own special touches. When you see cooking as a creative process, you can use it to express yourself, as a way to enjoy yourself and please others.

Be brave, be adventurous! But bear in mind that some immortally classic combinations, like pesto for example, are not necessarily improved by substituting, say, lemongrass and Roquefort for basil and Parmesan. Within the boundaries of tradition and sound judgement, there is room for individual expression. Your cooking style is based on who you are, and what you like to eat. Interestingly, many professional chefs still cite their mothers as the best cooks they know.

health notes

without meat, what are we missing out on?

When I tell someone I'm a vegetarian, I often get a reaction of concern – 'It must be so difficult to make sure you have a balanced diet,' or 'Isn't it hard to get enough protein?' The truth is that all the nutrients you need are abundant in vegetarian food. It's just important to eat a varied diet and to understand some basic nutrition facts.

PROTEIN

Protein is an essential part of the diet, but by cutting out meat, you're not in danger of being deprived of protein, unless you plan to live on leaves alone! Grains, pulses, eggs and dairy products are all good sources of protein. Protein should make up only 15 per cent of the diet so, provided your diet is varied, you will get enough. Try not to rely exclusively on cheese and eggs for protein – they're high in saturated fat which is linked to heart disease, and so should be eaten in moderation.

Proteins are made up of amino acids, of which there are 22 in all. The body manufactures most of these, but eight of them have to be acquired from the diet. Meat, fish, eggs and dairy produce contain all eight (they are 'complete proteins'), but soybeans* are the only non-animal complete protein source – one reason why tofu is such a prized vegetarian food. Rice, grains, pulses and nuts do not contain all eight, but by mixing these foods in the daily diet, for example, rice with beans, or peanut butter with bread, we make up complete proteins. Recent research shows that these complementary proteins do not have to be eaten together, as the body stores the amino acids short-term.

*Recent research suggests that eating large quantities of soy products can be harmful. As with eggs and cheese, it's best eaten in moderation. Fermentation may reduce harmful effects; so fermented soy products such as soy sauce, tempeh and miso are thought to be safer.

IRON

Iron plays an essential role in the circulatory system. It is used by the body to manufacture haemoglobin in your blood, carrying oxygen from the lungs to all the tissue cells and major organs in your body. Vitamin C, found in fresh fruit and vegetables, increases iron absorption.

Spinach, though it may have worked wonders for Popeye, is not a good source of iron. It does have a high iron content, but this is cancelled out by a high content of oxalic acid that binds with the iron to form an insoluble substance.

OTHER MINERALS

Meat and fish supply other essential minerals, especially calcium, zinc, selenium and iodine. Happily all are abundant in vegetarian foods.

B VITAMINS

B vitamins are essential for maintaining a healthy digestive and nervous system. Common food sources include yeast, wholegrain cereals, nuts, green vegetables, beans and pulses.

B12 is the only B vitamin that doesn't occur in plant foods (except seaweed). Only a very small amount is needed for good health and it can be found in eggs and dairy products. If you are a vegan, you should take this vitamin in supplement form, or incorporate B12-enriched foods into the diet.

OTHER VITAMINS

Vitamin D and Vitamin A are common in meat and fish as well as vegetarian foods. We make our own vitamin D when we are exposed to the sun. We get it from dairy products as well. Vitamin D, however, is not present in plant foods, so vegans are advised to take supplements.

Vitamin A is also found in dairy products, but the body also converts beta-carotene, found in orange-fleshed and dark green vegetables, into this essential vitamin.

OTHER ELEMENTS OF A HEALTHY DIET

Carbohydrate, fibre and fat are also essential to the diet on a daily basis.

The body converts carbohydrate into energy. The two main types of carbohydrate are starches and sugars. Starches are found in plant-based foods such as

rice, bread, potatoes, pasta, cereals and pulses. Unrefined types, such as whole wheat bread and brown rice, are the most valuable to the body, as they are rich in fibre and B vitamins.

Sugars which occur naturally in fruit and vegetables (as opposed to a jam doughnut) are valuable energy and fibre sources as well. These foods contain a whole range of other essential nutrients and should form a major part of everyday eating.

A moderate amount of fat is essential too – vegetable fats tend to be more unsaturated, which is a more healthy type of fat, than animal fats, which tend to be saturated (this includes cheese and eggs).

VEGETARIAN DAILY DIET

What a vegetarian should eat every day (as recommended by The Vegetarian Society) includes:

- 3 or 4 servings of cereals or potatoes.
- 4 or 5 servings of fruit and vegetables (though most nutritionists would recommend 5 to 6 servings).
- 2 to 3 servings of pulses, nuts and seeds.
- 2 servings of milk, cheese, eggs or soy products.

- A small amount of vegetable oil and butter.
- Some yeast extract such as Marmite or Vegemite, fortified with vitamin B12.

BEING VEGAN

Being a vegan means not consuming any animal by-products of any kind such as eggs, butter and milk – even honey. And it's not just about food. Vegans will not wear leather or anything else derived from animals. There are a surprisingly large number of everyday items which may use animal products as an ingredient or in the manufacturing process, including moisturizers, chewing gum, wine, beer, toothpaste and washing powder.

Vegans can still share the health benefits of a vegetarian diet despite these restrictions. However, it takes a lot more effort and consideration because there is a risk of malnutrition, especially vitamin B12 deficiency.

If you are considering becoming vegan, find out more about veganism first, and seek the advice of a nutritionist or community dietician.

the basics

RICE Rice should always be measured by volume, not by weight. Most varieties should be cooked in twice the volume of water: the rice then absorbs all the water. Long grain rice varieties include my favourite, basmati, which cooks in just 10–12 minutes and has a lovely nutty flavour and scent. Others are Thai fragrant rice – deliciously scented – and 'easy-cook' rice, which has been steam-treated to drive the nutrients back into the grain. Brown rice, also known as wholegrain rice, is not milled (only the husk is removed). It has a wonderful chewy texture and is high in B-vitamins and fibre. Camargue red rice, which cooks like wholegrain, can be difficult to find, but is full of flavour. Short grain varieties include sushi rice and risotto rice.

COUSCOUS Not to be confused with a grain, couscous is in fact a type of wheat pasta. It is delicious cold in salads or served hot with vegetable stews. It is easy to prepare: simply pour boiling water or stock over the couscous to cover, add a pinch of salt and let stand for 10–15 minutes until the liquid is absorbed. Alternatively, steam or microwave, then add a little butter. Fluff the grains with a fork.

BULGHUR Also known as cracked wheat, bulghur is probably best-known for its use in tabbouleh, a famous Lebanese dish. Bulghur is a good source of carbohydrate and will add bulk to vegetable dishes. Prepare in the same way as couscous, but let stand for 30 minutes.

POLENTA (CORNMEAL) Made from maize (corn), ground to a fine or coarse meal. It is fabulous with butter and Parmesan cheese, served soft or set and cut into pieces, then pan-grilled or fried. Do not use the variety that takes only 5 minutes to cook or the ready-made polenta that is vacuum-packed – both lack flavour and nuance. Polenta (uncooked) can used like breadcrumbs to give a crisp, crunchy coating to food (page 50). For cooking instructions for polenta, see page 72.

TOFU Made from soybeans, tofu (bean curd) is the best protein alternative to meat. Because it has no taste, tofu is usually marinated with strong, assertive flavours, such as garlic, ginger, and chillies, and either stir-fried or roasted. There are two types of tofu: silken tofu, which is soft and smooth, used mainly in milkshakes, cheesecakes, and cakes, and firm tofu, which has a more robust texture, suitable for stir-frying, deep-frying, and roasting. Firm tofu is also available smoked, but it doesn't need to be marinated, although it can taste artificial. Tofu will not keep long: if it smells sour, don't use it. If you don't use all the tofu at once, put the remainder in a bowl, cover with cold water, refrigerate, and use within 2 days, changing the water at least once.

Tempeh is another protein-rich food. Made from fermented soybeans, it has a firm texture, good flavor, and can be deep-fried, pan-fried, grilled or roasted. It is usually available frozen from natural food stores.

AUBERGINES A very versatile vegetable, the aubergine can be stuffed, roasted, char-grilled, fried or added to rice and pasta dishes, stews and bakes. Sprinkling them with salt is a traditional technique used to draw out any bitter juices. However, if you buy the modern, non-bitter variety you do not need to do this. But if you plan to sauté aubergines in oil, you may want to add a pinch of salt – it firms up the flesh so less oil will be absorbed. Salt will also make the aubergines crisper. Resist the temptation to add more oil, because some of the already absorbed oil will be released back into the pan as the aubergine cooks.

CHILLIES The intense fiery heat of chillies comes from capsaicin, a chemical that is present in varying degrees in all parts of the chilli. It is strongest in the membranes and the seeds, so take care when deseeding chillies. Wash your hands thoroughly afterwards and take particular care not to touch your eyes – capsaicin can sting. (I always wear rubber gloves when handling chillies.) Chillies are used extensively in Thai and Mexican cooking. As a general rule, green ones are milder than red and the smaller the chilli, the hotter it is. There are a few exceptions; the habañero and Scotch bonnet are both large, rippled and lantern-shaped, and often red, yellow or orange. Both are best avoided unless you really want to hit the ceiling.

OLIVE OIL Try to use the best extra virgin olive oil you can afford. A wildly expensive estate oil may be wasted in cooking – almost good enough to drink, it should be used in the raw for salads and dunking bread. For general cooking purposes, I buy 5-litre drums of reasonably priced extra virgin and decant it into a bottle with a cocktail spout for easy pouring. Like wines, olive oils have different characteristics of fruitiness and pepperiness, and what you love is an individual matter.

COOKING WITH WINE A splash of wine is a welcome addition to many recipes. The only rule of thumb is not to add it at the end of cooking, but at the start, to give the alcohol at least a few minutes to evaporate. My favourites are:

- Madeira (from the island bearing its name) is sweet and nutty – keep a bottle by the stove at all times.
- Port is a fortified wine and, in cooking, it imparts a deep wine flavour and dark colour.
- Vermouth isn't the finest of drinks, except as part of a dry martini, though it is the best fortified white wine for risotto. It can be substituted wherever white wine is required, as it doesn't oxidize and can be kept ready and waiting for splashing.

- Slightly less common are the two Japanese wines; mirin, a sweet wine for cooking only, and sake. Both, especially in combination, are wonderful in stir-fries and marinades, such as Roasted Teriyaki Tofu Steaks with Glazed Green Vegetables (page 68).

BREADCRUMBS Store-bought breadcrumbs taste stale and are generally bad value. Some bakeries will sell you a cheap bag of crumbs, but you can easily make your own by pulverizing stale cubes of bread in the food processor. You can then freeze them in bags. If you haven't got any stale bread, buy some crusty rolls or a small baguette, slice in half, and toast in the oven until crisp. Break into pieces and process in the machine.

basic recipes

vegetable stock

Using home-made vegetable stock creates a depth of flavour in soups and it is well worth going to the trouble of making. In fact, it's no trouble at all – just boil up a pan of water and pop in a quartered onion, sliced celery with leaves, a sliced carrot, some parsley and salt and simmer for 30 minutes. And there you have it. But you needn't buy vegetables specifically for stock. Always save the water you've used to steam, blanch or boil vegetables: cool and store in a sealed bag in the freezer and you'll always have some to hand. Alternatively, boil up vegetable off-cuts. Stock options – good and bad – are:

- Especially good; scallion and leek greens (well washed), broccoli and cauliflower stems, celery leaves, fresh pea pods, herb stems, fennel tops and tomato skins.
- Not so good; onion skins, cabbage, potatoes and pepper seeds.

I have to admit I regularly succumb to the convenience of vegetable stock cubes or granules. Read the label and go organic or without 'flavourings' or additives.

beans

Freshly cooked beans do taste better than canned, but not always infinitely superior. While it's hardly back-breaking to throw some dried beans in a bowl of water and leave them overnight, it does require a little forward planning and possibly takes away a little of the spontaneity – so I've given both options in the recipes. If you are using dried beans, remember:

- Lentils DO NOT need soaking, but should be rinsed before cooking.
- Rinse beans first and check for pebbles or rogue beans.
- Put the beans in a bowl with 3 times their volume of cold water. Leave for at least 12 hours, or overnight in the refrigerator if it's warm in the kitchen.
- Drain off the soaking water and boil the beans in plenty of fresh water. Let them boil furiously for 10 minutes, then add salt. (Adding salt before this will toughen the skins.)
- Skim off any foam that forms on the surface of the water.
- Beans will cook in between 30 minutes and 2 hours, depending on the type of bean and its age.

ALL RECIPES SERVE FOUR

basic tomato sauce

2 tablespoons olive oil

1 onion, chopped

3 garlic cloves, chopped

500 g canned chopped tomatoes

1 teaspoon balsamic vinegar

1 teaspoon sugar

salt and pepper

Heat the oil in a frying pan. Add the onion and fry gently until translucent. Add the garlic and fry until fragrant. Add the remaining ingredients and simmer gently for 15–20 minutes.

Optional extra: chopped chilli (added with the onion), a splash of red wine, Madeira, port or vermouth (added with tomatoes) or fresh torn basil leaves (added in the last minute of cooking).

basic cheese sauce

2 tablespoons butter

2 tablespoons plain flour

300 ml milk

100 g grated sharp-flavoured hard cheese such as Cheddar or Gruyère

Melt the butter in a frying pan set over a low heat. Sprinkle with flour. Cook, stirring, for 2 minutes.

Meanwhile warm the milk in the microwave or in a saucepan. Gradually pour the milk into the flour mixture, stirring constantly. When thickened, stir in the grated cheese and stir until smooth. Serve immediately.

Optional extras: infuse the milk by simmering it for a few minutes with a bay leaf, half a sliced onion and a garlic clove.
Alternatively, at the same time as the cheese, add 2 teaspoons mustard, 2 teaspoons horseradish or ½ teaspoon asafoetida and ½ teaspoon ground turmeric.

pesto

a large bunch of basil

100 g pine nuts, lightly toasted in a dry frying pan

3 garlic cloves

50 g grated Parmesan cheese

6 tablespoons olive oil

sea salt and freshly ground black pepper

Put the basil, pine nuts, garlic and Parmesan in a food processor and blend. Drizzle in the olive oil little by little. Season to taste.

Optional extras: pesto is one of those sublime combinations that really shouldn't be interfered with. An exception is Smoked Chilli Pesto, made with smoked chilli and pimentón – pimentón is smoked paprika; if you can't find it, use ordinary paprika. Before processing, soak 1 dried smoked chilli in hot water, remove the seeds and chop the flesh. Add to the pesto, with 2 teaspoons mild pimentón, before processing.

basic vinaigrette

It's a matter of personal taste, but use a ratio of 3 parts olive oil to 2 parts balsamic, cider or wine vinegar. Using a mortar and pestle, mash 1 garlic clove and 1 teaspoon coarse salt to a smooth purée. Whisk in 2 tablespoons vinegar, pepper and a little sugar. Gradually whisk in 3 tablespoons olive oil until emulsified. Alternatively, crush the garlic clove and shake all the ingredients in a screw-top jar.

Optional extras: add 1–2 teaspoons mustard and ½ teaspoon dried herbs de Provence or a small handful of fresh chopped herbs, especially dill. Alternatively, use fresh lemon juice instead of vinegar.

guacamole

2 very ripe avocados

juice of 1 lime

sea salt

Scoop the flesh from the avocados into a bowl. Add lime juice and salt and mash with a fork or potato masher. If made ahead of time, reserve 1 avocado stone and leave it in the guacamole until time to serve. Miraculously, it will stop the guacamole discolouring.

Optional extras: add 1 crushed garlic clove, 1 chopped chilli or a few dashes of Tabasco sauce, 1 small, finely chopped onion, 1 chopped tomato and a small bunch of coriander, chopped.

the store cupboard

THE FOLLOWING ITEMS, MOST USED IN THIS BOOK, ARE ALL USEFUL TO HAVE ON HAND FOR VEGETARIAN COOKING.

OILS AND VINEGARS

extra virgin olive oil

sunflower oil

sesame oil

truffle oil (drizzle on all things mushroomy just before serving)

white/red wine vinegar

balsamic vinegar

cider vinegar

rice vinegar

sushi vinegar (makes a lovely light salad dressing on its own)

SEASONINGS AND FLAVOURINGS

vegetable stock cubes or powder

coarse sea salt

fine sea salt (for baking)

Japanese soy sauce, tamari or shoyu (fermented dark soy sauce)

light soy sauce

Thai sweet chilli sauce

Tabasco sauce

chilli paste, such as harissa or sambal oelek

vegetarian Worcestershire sauce

tamarind pulp

COOKING WINES

red, white and Madeira

port (especially ruby port, as it's relatively inexpensive and has a deep colour)

vermouth

mirin and sake (see Cooking with wine, page 11)

NUTS AND SEEDS

sesame seeds

poppy seeds

pumpkin seeds

pine nuts

salted, roasted peanuts

ground almonds

vacuum-packed chestnuts

PICKLES AND DRIED ITEMS

dried fruits such as raisins, sultanas, apricots, cranberries and prunes

pickled onions

capers in salt or vinegar

high-quality olives such as kalamata

pickled jalapeño pepper slices

dried smoked chillies, such as chipotles

dried porcini mushrooms

dried shiitake mushrooms

SPREADS, SAUCES AND SWEET THINGS

honey

golden syrup

vanilla essence

rose water

orange flower water

marmalade

berry, plum or apricot jam

lemon or orange curd

peanut butter

unsweetened cocoa powder

vegetarian gelatine alternative

sugar: caster, soft brown, demerara and unrefined icing sugar

BAKING, PASTA, GRAINS AND PULSES

plain flour

strong bread flour

baking powder

bicarbonate of soda

wheat germ

masa harina

cornflour

polenta

porridge oats

rice: basmati, arborio (for risotto) and sushi rice

bulghur

pasta

couscous

noodles: rice stick, rice vermicelli, egg noodles

flour tortillas

lentils (especially Puy)

dried beans

HERBS AND SPICES

bay leaves

oregano

saffron threads

ground turmeric

mild chilli powder (generally a mix with garlic, cumin and oregano)

cayenne pepper

dried chilli flakes

paprika

pimentón (smoked paprika)

cloves: ground and whole

cinnamon: ground and sticks or bark

whole nutmegs

vanilla pods

cumin: ground and seeds

coriander seeds

cardamom pods

whole fenugreek

asafoetida (pungent, onion-scented spice)

sumac (deep red, citrus-flavoured spice, excellent sprinkled on salad)

FOOD IN CANS

refried beans

chickpeas

butter beans

pinto or borlotti beans

corn kernels

coconut milk

coconut cream

peeled plum tomatoes

chopped tomatoes

MISCELLANEOUS

mayonnaise

mustard: English, Dijon wholegrain

creamed horseradish

recommended equipment

chef's knife and sharpening steel – buy a large soft-alloy knife. The best is an alloy with a soft metal such as molybdenum, vanadium and stainless steel. It has a razor-sharp edge which needs sharpening regularly.

vegetable paring knife

bread knife

food processor with chopping blade, slicing blade and grater.

blender

hand blender for puréeing soups.

hand whisk or electric hand mixer.

large wok with dome lid – indispensable, not only for stir-frying, but also deep-frying and steaming. Traditional woks, made from iron or carbon steel with a wooden handle (a design perfected over 2000 years ago), are rounded on the bottom, and therefore only suitable for cooking over a gas flame. If your heat source is electric, AGA or Rayburn, opt for a modern version with a partly flat base.

To season a new traditional wok, scrub well, rinse and dry. Wipe with vegetable oil and place over a low flame for 10 minutes. Cool, wipe away the burnt film, and repeat the process until it wipes clean. Never scrub when washing, but wipe clean with hot water and a sponge, and rub with vegetable oil after drying. If the wok does get scrubbed or becomes rusty, simply season again.

wok scoop – a shovel-like implement, ideal for stir-frying.

long tongs

fish slice or spatula

potato masher

bamboo steamer – can be used in the wok or on top of a pan. These are very cheap and will need replacing every so often, as they absorb flavours.

bamboo or wire sieve or flat slotted spoon.

large frying pan – either non-stick coated or well seasoned cast iron.

heavy-based saucepans in a variety of sizes.

large cast iron stove-top grill pan – if you can find one that fits over two gas burners, so much the better.

large mortar and pestle

muffin tins – I have discovered a remarkable silicon-based rubberized muffin maker that eliminates the need for greasing. It makes 6 plump muffins that just pop out. Available in kitchen shops or visit www.paton-calvert.co.uk. or www.lakelandlimited.com.

springform cake tin – 24 cm diameter with removable base and sides.

loaf tin – 400 g capacity.

mince pie tins – I recommend Prestige brand non-stick.

large and medium baking sheets

power shake

We must eat and drink to 'break' the 'fast' since last night's dinner. However, many of us don't even wake up hungry, or we're too busy getting ready for work or feeding the family. It's likely we'll put off eating until late morning, when our stomachs rumble loudly and we reach for a delicious but unhealthy sweet pastry. Instead, spare just five minutes in the morning to make a nutritious, filling shake to kick-start your day.

about 150 g prepared fruit, such as berries, mango, banana, papaya, peach, apricot, melon or kiwifruit

250 ml low-fat plain yoghurt

250 ml fruit juice, such as orange, apple, pineapple or cranberry

50 g ground almonds

2 tablespoons honey

3–4 tablespoons wheatgerm

a pinch of ground cinnamon

SERVES 2

Put all the ingredients in a blender and blend until smooth. Pour into glasses and serve with a straw. This shake will keep in the refrigerator for 2 days.

VARIATIONS

- Use 100 g silken tofu instead of ground almonds.

- Replace the fruit juice with low-fat milk, soy milk or unsweetened coconut milk.

- Omit the wheatgerm and use porridge oats instead.

- Add other flavourings before blending, such as 1 teaspoon pure vanilla essence, a dash of almond essence or 2 teaspoons grated fresh ginger.

- For a thick shake, add ice cubes before blending.

muffins

Nothing beats a fresh batch of home-baked muffins for an extra-special treat (with butter if you dare) and a cup of steaming coffee or tea. Though they're best eaten hot from the oven, the muffins can be made the night before, cooled, stored in an airtight container, then reheated before serving.

lemon poppy seed muffins

250 g plain flour

1 teaspoon baking powder

¼ teaspoon fine sea salt

3 tablespoons poppy seeds

200 g sugar

2 eggs, lightly beaten

grated zest of 2 lemons and juice of 1

65 g butter, melted, or 80 ml sunflower oil

1 teaspoon pure vanilla essence

125 ml low-fat plain yoghurt

a 6-hole or 12-hole muffin tin, well greased

MAKES 6 LARGE OR 12 SMALL MUFFINS

Sift the flour and baking powder into a bowl and stir in the salt and poppy seeds. Add the remaining ingredients and fold everything together until just blended; do not beat or overmix. Spoon the batter into the prepared tin and bake in a preheated oven at 180°C (350°F) Gas 4 for 20–30 minutes, until golden and firm. Let cool in the tin for 10 minutes, then turn out onto a wire rack.

VARIATIONS

- Blueberry Muffins: omit the poppy seeds, lemon zest and juice. Fold 200 g blueberries into the batter.

- Fruit and Nut Muffins: omit the poppy seeds, lemon zest and juice. Add 75 g dried mixed fruit and 75 g chopped nuts to the batter.

corn muffins

75 g plain flour

2 teaspoons baking powder

1 teaspoon fine sea salt

300 g coarse polenta or yellow cornmeal

100 g caster sugar

2 eggs, lightly beaten

100 g butter, melted (125 ml)

175 ml milk

150 g fresh corn kernels or canned, rinsed and drained

a 6-hole or 12-hole muffin tin, well greased

MAKES 6 LARGE OR 12 SMALL MUFFINS

Heat the prepared muffin tin in a preheated oven at 190°C (375°F) Gas 5 for 5 minutes (this will make the outside of the muffins crisp). Meanwhile, sift the flour and baking powder into a bowl and stir in the salt, polenta or cornmeal and sugar. Add the eggs, melted butter and milk, then mix until smooth. Add the corn and mix. Spoon the batter into the hot muffin tin and bake at the same temperature for 20–30 minutes, until golden and firm. Let cool in the tin for 10 minutes, then turn out onto a wire rack.

VARIATION

- Chilli Corn Muffins: reduce the sugar to 1 tablespoon. Add 1 teaspoon chopped chillies or 50 g chopped red peppers.

A stack of fluffy, American-style pancakes in the morning will keep you fuelled for hours. This recipe is based on one from *The Joy of Cooking* — and, in my opinion, the batter can't be bettered. Make it before bedtime and leave it overnight in the fridge. In the morning, you'll have a breakfast feast in minutes.

american pancakes

250 g plain flour

2 teaspoons baking powder

1 teaspoon sea salt

3 tablespoons sugar

250 ml milk

2 eggs, lightly beaten

50 g unsalted butter, melted, plus extra for cooking

MAPLE BUTTER SYRUP

80 ml maple syrup

25 g unsalted butter

MAKES 8–12, SERVES 4

Sift the flour, baking powder, salt and sugar into a bowl. Mix the milk, eggs and the 50 g melted butter in a large jug, then add the flour mixture and mix quickly to make a batter (don't worry about lumps – they're good). Alternatively, make the batter in a bowl and transfer to a jug.

Heat a cast iron frying pan or flat-surfaced griddle until medium hot, grease lightly with extra butter and pour in the batter in batches to make rounds, 8–10 cm diameter. Cook for 1–2 minutes or until bubbles form on top of the pancakes and the underside is golden, then flip each one over and cook for 1 minute. Keep the pancakes warm in the oven while you cook the remaining batches.

Heat the maple syrup and butter together in a small saucepan or microwave, then stack the pancakes on warmed plates and pour over the buttery syrup.

COTTAGE CHEESE PANCAKES

Make the batter as above, then stir in 8 tablespoons of cottage cheese. Proceed with the recipe. Serve with fresh berries, cherry or blackcurrant jam and crème fraîche, sour cream or thick yoghurt.

A favourite dish from my home in the South-western United States. Assembling the burritos is quick and simple, and you can save extra time in the morning if you make the salsa the night before or use a good-quality ready-made salsa – perfect even for the sleepiest of cooks.

breakfast burrito

To make the burritos, put each tortilla on a large sheet of foil, spread with the mashed beans and top with the cheese. Gather the foil and fold it at the top to seal, keeping the tortilla relatively flat. Put in a preheated oven at 200°C (400°F) Gas 6 for 7–10 minutes, until the cheese has just melted and the beans and tortilla are heated through, but not crisp.

Meanwhile, beat the eggs, milk, chilli, oregano, salt and pepper in a bowl. Heat the oil in a non-stick frying pan, add the egg mixture and cook, stirring frequently, until just set. Remove the burritos from the oven, open the foil parcel and spoon the scrambled eggs on top. Reseal and return to the oven to keep them warm.

When ready to eat, unwrap the burritos on a plate and, using the foil to help, roll each one into a cylinder. Top with salsa, guacamole and a spoonful of thick yoghurt.

4 large flour tortillas, 20 cm diameter

400 g canned refried beans, or canned borlotti or pinto beans, rinsed, drained and mashed

200 g mature Cheddar cheese, grated

6 eggs

2 tablespoons milk

1 teaspoon mild chilli powder

a pinch of dried oregano

1 tablespoon olive oil

sea salt and freshly ground black pepper

TO SERVE

Pickled Jalapeño Salsa or Salsa Fresca (page 62–3)

Guacamole (page 13)

thick plain yoghurt

SERVES 4

japanese omelette

This technique for making a very light omelette was shown to me by a Japanese friend. The end result is a delicate *millefeuille* – thin layers of egg, deeply flavoured with shiitake mushrooms. This four-person omelette is perfect for brunch or a lazy weekend breakfast. If you are feeling particularly hungry, serve the omelette with grilled vine tomatoes, slices of ripe avocado and slices of hot buttered toast – bliss.

6 fresh or dried shiitake
mushrooms

3 teaspoons vegetable oil

8 eggs

125 ml vegetable stock or
mushroom soaking liquid
(see method)

1–1½ tablespoons light soy sauce

1 tablespoon mirin (Japanese
sweet rice wine) or 1 teaspoon
sugar

28 cm non-stick frying pan

SERVES 4

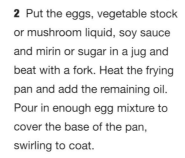

1 If using dried shiitakes, soak them in hot water for 30 minutes, then drain, reserving 125 ml of the liquid. Finely slice the mushrooms. Heat 2 teaspoons of the oil in the pan, add the mushrooms and sauté for 2 minutes, until golden. Drain on kitchen paper and set aside.

2 Put the eggs, vegetable stock or mushroom liquid, soy sauce and mirin or sugar in a jug and beat with a fork. Heat the frying pan and add the remaining oil. Pour in enough egg mixture to cover the base of the pan, swirling to coat.

3 Sprinkle with a few mushrooms, then cook until the egg is barely set, but not dry. Using a heatproof, non-metal spatula or fish slice, loosen the edges and roll up the egg layer from one side of the pan to the other. Do not remove.

4 Pour in more egg mixture as before, letting it touch the rolled omelette. Add a few mushrooms and cook until the egg is barely set. Starting with the cooked omelette, roll it to the other side of the pan – as you do this the new egg layer with roll up with it.

5 Repeat, layering and rolling until all the mushroom and egg mixture has been used. The finished omelette should be quite thick with many rolled layers.

6 Slide the omelette out of the pan onto a large sheet of foil. Roll up into a long sausage shape and scrunch the foil at the ends to seal. Let stand for 5–10 minutes.

7 Unwrap and remove the foil, then cut the omelette crossways into 4 or 8 pieces and serve.

celeriac, saffron and orange soup
with parsley gremolata

An elegant, rich soup. It can be made dairy-free for vegans – use olive oil instead of butter and leave out the yoghurt or crème fraîche. Although the parsley gremolata is optional, it will lift both colour and flavour.

Heat the butter or oil in a saucepan, add the onion and cook until softened. Add the celeriac and potato, if using, cover and cook for 10 minutes, stirring occasionally. Add the remaining ingredients. Bring to the boil, then simmer for 20 minutes until the vegetables are tender. Using a hand-held stick blender, purée until smooth. Alternatively, purée in a blender or food processor, in batches if necessary.

To make the gremolata, if using, put all the ingredients in a food processor or spice grinder and purée until smooth. Alternatively, use a mortar and pestle.

To serve, ladle the soup into warmed bowls and spoon over the gremolata and crème fraîche or yoghurt.

2 tablespoons butter or olive oil

1 large onion, chopped

1 celeriac, about 750 g, peeled and cut into cubes (make up the weight with potatoes, if necessary)

1 litre vegetable stock

½ teaspoon saffron strands, lightly ground with a mortar and pestle

1 tablespoon honey

grated zest and juice of 1 large orange

sea salt and freshly ground black pepper

crème fraîche or thick plain yoghurt, to serve

PARSLEY GREMOLATA (OPTIONAL)

1 garlic clove

1 teaspoon coarse sea salt

a handful of fresh flat leaf parsley

2 tablespoons olive oil

SERVES 4

soups & salads

I've lost count of how many times I've been told, 'this is the best gazpacho I've ever tasted'. Ice-cold and enhanced with avocado, lime, cumin and chilli, this soup is refreshingly hard to beat on a hot summer's day. If you have the foresight, freeze coriander leaves in ice cubes and use them to give your soup a decorative finish.

mexican gazpacho

2 garlic cloves

1 teaspoon coarse sea salt

30 cm cucumber, coarsely chopped

1 yellow pepper, deseeded and coarsely chopped

2 celery stalks, coarsely chopped

4 ripe tomatoes, coarsely chopped

1 red onion, coarsely chopped

1 litre fresh tomato juice

2 teaspoons cumin seeds, pan-toasted

1 teaspoon mild chilli powder

1 ripe avocado, halved and pitted

juice of 2 limes

freshly ground black pepper

TO SERVE

coriander leaves set in ice cubes or chopped coriander

SERVES 6

Using a mortar and pestle, pound the garlic with the salt until puréed. Put the cucumber, pepper, celery, tomato and onion in a bowl, add the puréed garlic and mix well. Transfer half of the mixture to a food processor and pulse until chopped but still slightly chunky. Pour into a bowl. Purée the remaining mixture until smooth, then add to the bowl. Mix in the tomato juice, cumin, chilli powder and freshly ground black pepper to taste.

Chill for several hours or overnight, until very cold. If short of time, put the soup in the freezer for 30 minutes to chill.

Cut the avocado into small cubes, toss in the lime juice until well coated, then stir into the gazpacho.

To serve, ladle the soup into chilled bowls, then add a few ice cubes or sprinkle with chopped coriander.

shiitake and field mushroom soup

with madeira and thyme

This soup is simplicity itself. There may seem to be a lot of mushrooms in it, but they shrink considerably when cooked and release their flavourful juices into the aromatic broth.

25 g butter

1 medium onion, chopped

2 garlic cloves, chopped

250 g shiitake mushrooms, torn or chopped into big chunks

250 g open-capped mushrooms or portobello mushrooms, torn or chopped into big chunks

150 ml Madeira wine or dry sherry

500 ml vegetable stock

a bunch of fresh thyme, tied with string

sea salt and freshly ground black pepper

TO SERVE

double cream

chopped parsley

freshly ground black pepper

SERVES 4

Melt the butter in a large saucepan, add the onion and cook over a low heat until softened and translucent. Add the garlic, mushrooms, salt and pepper. Increase the heat, cover and cook, stirring occasionally, until the mushrooms have softened and their juices been released, about 5 minutes.

Pour in the stock and Madeira or sherry and drop in the bundle of thyme. Bring to the boil, then cover and simmer for 15 minutes. Remove the thyme. Using a hand-held stick blender, coarsely purée the mixture. Alternatively, purée in a blender or food processor, in batches if necessary. Ladle into warmed bowls, top with a swirl of cream, chopped parsley and lots of black pepper, then serve.

lentil, coconut and wilted spinach soup

Puy lentils are grown in France and have achieved a regal status among pulses. They have a distinctive flavour and, unlike other lentils, hold their shape when cooked. If unavailable, use green or brown lentils. Add the spinach at the end: it doesn't need cooking.

150 g Puy lentils

1 litre vegetable stock

1 onion, chopped

2 fat garlic cloves, chopped

2 teaspoons ground cumin

100 g creamed coconut, chopped and dissolved in 150 ml boiling water

or 250 ml canned coconut milk

2–3 tablespoons dark soy sauce

4 small handfuls of baby spinach, about 50 g

sea salt and freshly ground black pepper

SERVES 4

Rinse the lentils, then put in a large saucepan and add enough cold water just to cover. Boil for 10 minutes, then add the remaining ingredients, except the spinach. Reduce the heat and simmer for 20–30 minutes or until the lentils are tender.

Put a small handful of the spinach in 4 warmed bowls and ladle the hot soup on top. The heat from the soup will wilt the leaves. Serve with warm flatbread, such as pita or naan.

This hybrid Thai coleslaw is based on the classic *som tum*, usually made from grated green papaya (when unripe, the fruit is firm, crunchy and perfect for grating). Alas, green papaya is not the easiest ingredient to find, so I've used red cabbage instead. The word 'coleslaw' comes from *koolsla* – Dutch for 'cabbage salad'. I merged these two classic dishes in a salad with a delicious new twist.

thai coleslaw

100 g green beans, trimmed

200 g finely shredded red or white cabbage

3 plum tomatoes, halved lengthways, deseeded and sliced

4 spring onions, sliced

50 g roasted peanuts, coarsely ground

4 cup-shaped lettuce leaves, to serve (optional)

DRESSING

a handful of fresh coriander

2 red chillies, deseeded

2 garlic cloves, chopped

2 tablespoons light soy sauce

2 tablespoons freshly squeezed lime juice

2 tablespoons palm sugar or soft brown sugar

SERVES 4

To make the dressing, reserve a few coriander leaves, then put the rest in a blender or food processor. Add the chillies, garlic, soy sauce, lime juice and sugar and blend until smooth. Set aside.

Blanch the beans in boiling water for 2 minutes, then refresh in cold water. Mix the cabbage, beans, tomatoes and spring onions in a bowl. Pour the dressing on top, toss well to coat and let marinate for about 30 minutes. Spoon into bowls lined with the lettuce leaves, if using, sprinkle with the ground peanuts and the reserved coriander leaves, then serve.

char-grilled asparagus and leaf salad

with sesame-soy dressing

During its short season, I feast on asparagus nearly every day. I think char-grilling is the best way of cooking the spears – it seals in their sweet, earthy flavour. Turn this salad into a main dish by adding boiled eggs.

3 tablespoons sesame seeds

2 bunches of asparagus, about 24 spears

2 tablespoons dark soy sauce

2 tablespoons balsamic vinegar

5 tablespoons olive oil, plus extra for brushing

300 g mixed salad leaves, such as rocket, watercress and spinach

SERVES 4–6

Lightly toast the sesame seeds in a dry frying pan, stirring frequently, until golden and popping. Transfer to a bowl and let cool.

Wash the asparagus and cut off any tough stalks. Brush with olive oil. Heat a stove-top grill pan until very hot, add the asparagus (in batches, if necessary) and cook, turning occasionally, until bright green, blistered and slightly charred, about 5–7 minutes (depending on thickness).

Put the toasted sesame seeds, soy sauce and balsamic vinegar in a bowl and gradually whisk in the oil until emulsified. To assemble, put the salad leaves on a platter, arrange the asparagus on top, drizzle with the sesame dressing and serve.

1 kg baby new potatoes,
scrubbed

4 spring onions,
chopped

3 tablespoons capers

125 g crème fraîche

125 g low-fat plain
yoghurt

1 teaspoon finely grated
lemon zest

½ teaspoon saffron
strands, soaked in
1 teaspoon hot water

sea salt and freshly
ground black pepper

snipped chives, to serve

SERVES 4–6

Cook the potatoes in boiling salted
water for 15–20 minutes or until tender,
then drain and let cool.

Mix the remaining ingredients in a bowl,
then add the potatoes and turn until
well coated. Cover and chill for at least
30 minutes to let the flavours develop.
Serve sprinkled with snipped chives.

saffron potato salad

No ordinary potato salad: this one is cloaked in
a luscious, creamy dressing flavoured with saffron.
Serve it as part of a salad feast: with Puy lentils
dressed in lemon juice, onion and herbs; and a
green salad tossed in a sweet-and-sour vinaigrette.

1 cos lettuce, outer
leaves removed, or
2 small lettuce hearts

freshly grated Parmesan
cheese, to serve

CROUTONS

2 thick slices white
bread, cubed

1 tablespoon olive oil

DRESSING

2 eggs

4 tablespoons freshly
grated Parmesan cheese

3 tablespoons white
wine vinegar

2 teaspoons vegetarian
Worcestershire sauce

1 tablespoon snipped
chives (optional)

4 tablespoons olive oil

sea salt and freshly
ground black pepper

SERVES 4–6

This classic salad never seems to lose its appeal and is constantly being updated. The original recipe calls for barely cooked eggs, which many vegetarians find unpalatable and should be avoided if you are pregnant, ill, very young or elderly. Boiled eggs, cooked until the yolks are just set, make a fantastic dressing, and who needs anchovies when you can use a vegetarian Worcestershire sauce? If unavailable, add an extra pinch of salt instead.

caesar salad

To make the croutons, put the cubes of bread in a bowl, drizzle with the olive oil and toss until evenly coated. Tip onto a baking sheet and bake in a preheated oven at 190°C (375°F) Gas 5 until golden and crisp on all sides, about 10 minutes. Check the bread occasionally while cooking, so it doesn't burn. Let cool.

To make the dressing, put the eggs in a saucepan of cold water and bring to the boil. Cook for 5–6 minutes, then drain immediately and cool under cold running water. Peel the eggs when cold, then put in a small bowl and mash with a fork. Add the remaining dressing ingredients, except the oil, and whisk thoroughly. Gradually add the oil – a little at a time – whisking until emulsified.

Tear the lettuce into pieces and put in a large bowl, pour over the dressing and toss until well coated. Top with the croutons, sprinkle with Parmesan and serve.

warm chickpea salad

with spiced mushrooms

This main-course salad was inspired by Middle Eastern cuisine, where beans, yoghurt and mint are widely used. Make this dish more substantial by serving it on a bed of couscous or bulghur wheat. The convenience of canned chickpeas may appeal if you don't have time to soak, then cook the dried variety. You won't notice any difference in taste.

150 g dried chickpeas or 400 g canned chickpeas

3 tablespoons olive oil

300 g button mushrooms

2 garlic cloves, chopped

1 red chilli, deseeded and chopped

2 teaspoons ground cumin

juice of 1 lemon

175 ml Greek or thick plain yoghurt

a large handful of mint leaves, chopped

250 g baby spinach leaves

sea salt and freshly ground black pepper

SERVES 4

If using dried chickpeas, soak them overnight in cold water, then rinse and drain. Put in a saucepan, cover with water and bring to the boil. Cook for 10 minutes, then add salt, reduce the heat and simmer for 1–1½ hours, until tender. If using canned chickpeas, rinse and drain.

Heat 2 tablespoons of the oil a frying pan. Add the mushrooms, season with salt and cook until softened. Reduce the heat, then add the garlic, chilli and chickpeas. Fry for 2 minutes, then add the cumin and half the lemon juice. Cook until the juices in the pan evaporate, then set aside.

Put the yoghurt in a bowl, then add the chopped mint and the remaining lemon juice and oil. Add salt and pepper and mix until blended. Divide the spinach between 4 plates or put on a serving platter, add the chickpea and mushroom mixture, then pour the yoghurt dressing over the top and serve.

2 red peppers, halved
and deseeded

2 yellow peppers, halved
and deseeded

500 g ripe plum tomatoes

4 tablespoons red wine
vinegar

2 garlic cloves, crushed
to a paste with coarse
sea salt

freshly ground black
pepper

125 ml extra virgin olive
oil, plus extra for
drizzling

2 tablespoons capers

75 g black olives, pitted

1 small or ½ large loaf
day-old ciabatta, cut
coarsely into cubes

a bunch of fresh basil,
leaves, torn

SERVES 4–6

Make this sumptuous salad with flavourful, deep-red tomatoes. The bread drinks up the rich, summer flavours of the tomato and roasted pepper dressing. It's important to use a crusty, firm-crumbed bread, such as ciabatta, country-style or sourdough, so it doesn't revert to a dough-like state.

tuscan panzanella

Put the peppers cut-side down on a baking sheet and grill until blistered and charred. Transfer to a plastic bag, seal and let cool (the steam will loosen the skin, making it easier to peel). Scrape off the skin, then cut the peppers into strips, reserving any juice.

Halve the tomatoes and scoop out the cores and seeds over a bowl to catch the juice. Purée the cores and seeds in a blender, then press the extra juice through a sieve into the bowl. Discard the pulp and seeds. Cut the tomato halves into strips.

Put the tomato juice, vinegar, garlic and freshly ground black pepper in a bowl. Gradually add the 125 ml extra virgin olive oil, whisking until blended.

Mix the strips of peppers and tomatoes in a bowl, add the capers, olives, ciabatta and basil and mix. Add the dressing, toss well to coat, then set aside for 1 hour to develop the flavours. Drizzle with extra olive oil and serve.

To make the latkes, peel the potatoes, then grate on the coarse side of a box grater or in a food processor. Transfer to a sieve and let drain. Press excess moisture out of the potatoes (or they will 'spit' when fried) and put them in a bowl. Finely chop the onion and add to the bowl. Add the lemon zest and juice, flour, baking powder and salt and mix well. Return to the sieve – liquid will continue to drain out of the mixture while you prepare to cook the latkes.

Heat about 5 mm depth of olive oil in a frying pan. Add rounded tablespoons of the mixture and flatten slightly; don't overcrowd the pan. Fry for 2–3 minutes on each side until golden and crisp. Remove with a slotted spoon and drain on crumpled kitchen paper. Keep the latkes warm in the oven while you cook the rest.

To make the avocado crème, scoop the avocado flesh into a bowl and mash with a fork. Add the remaining ingredients and beat until smooth, then serve with the latkes.

NOTE: Latkes make excellent canapés. Fry teaspoons of the mixture as described above, then serve topped with the avocado crème and coriander leaves. Makes about 50.

2 large potatoes, about 750 g

1 small onion

grated zest of 1 lemon

2 teaspoons freshly squeezed lemon juice

4 tablespoons plain flour

¼ teaspoon baking powder

1 teaspoon sea salt

olive oil, for frying

GINGERED AVOCADO CRÈME

1 large ripe avocado, halved and pitted

juice of 1 lime

1–2 teaspoons finely grated ginger

½ teaspoon crushed garlic

1 red chilli, deseeded and finely chopped, or 1 tablespoon chilli sauce

1 tablespoon light soy sauce

2 tablespoons thick plain yoghurt

lemon potato latkes

with gingered avocado crème

Though rather indulgent, fried potato cakes are worth every wicked mouthful. Keep them small and they'll cook in a matter of minutes. Eat them as soon as possible or reheat later in a very hot oven for 5 minutes. With this spicy avocado accompaniment or one of the dipping sauces on page 59, latkes taste even better.

MAKES 20–24, SERVES 4

Put the flour and salt in a large bowl and make a well in the centre. Crumble the yeast into a jug, mix to a smooth paste with 4 tablespoons warm water, then top up to 250 ml. Pour into the well and add the 2 tablespoons oil. Gradually work in the flour to make a soft but not sticky dough. If it is too dry or too sticky, add extra water or flour, 1 tablespoon at a time.

Turn out onto a floured surface and knead thoroughly for 10 minutes, until smooth and elastic. Put in an oiled bowl and turn the dough until shiny all over. Cover with a damp tea towel and let rise in a warm place until doubled in size – about 30 minutes.

Meanwhile, to make the topping, cut the onions in half, from top to bottom, and thickly slice lengthways. Heat the oil in a frying pan, add the onions and fry until golden. Add the salt, sugar and wine and cook until the onions have caramelized, about 3–5 minutes.

Sprinkle the polenta or cornmeal onto a baking sheet. This will prevent the focaccia from sticking and will make the base crisp.

Knock down the risen dough with your knuckles, then turn out onto the prepared baking sheet and flatten into a round, about 2 cm thick. Top with the caramelized onions and Gruyère. Cover and let rise as before for 30 minutes (no longer or the bread will be hard and dry).

Bake in a preheated oven at 220°C (425°F) Gas 7 for 30–40 minutes, until golden. Let cool slightly, then cut into wedges and serve.

500 g strong white bread flour

1 teaspoon sea salt

15 g fresh yeast*

2 tablespoons olive oil, plus extra for greasing

3 tablespoons polenta or cornmeal

CHEESE AND ONION TOPPING

500 g red onions

2 tablespoons olive oil

a large pinch of sea salt

1 teaspoon sugar

75 ml white or red wine

100 g grated Gruyère cheese

SERVES 4–6

* To use easy-blend dried yeast, mix one 7 g sachet with the flour and salt. Make a well in the centre, add 250 ml warm water, then proceed with the recipe.

caramelized onion and gruyère

focaccia

For a long time, I was afraid of making bread, thinking it too laborious. Then, a few years ago, I made a New Year's resolution to make a loaf twice a week and in doing so overcame my fear. I find that kneading is a good stress-buster. It also keeps my arms in great shape and warms me up on a cold day. This is the simplest of loaves – almost like pizza with a lush topping. It's a meal in itself or is perfect with soup.

An explosion of flavour and texture: the crisp coating protects the deep-fried mushrooms so they are juicy, not greasy. Vary the cheese filling if you can't find dried porcini mushrooms – add a little finely chopped red chilli or a mixture of chopped herbs. These balls make a brilliant appetizer or delicious party food.

stuffed polenta mushrooms

32 closed-cap mushrooms, about 2.5–5 cm diameter

75 g polenta or cornmeal

3 tablespoons sesame seeds

1 teaspoon sea salt

2 eggs

sunflower oil, for frying

CREAM CHEESE FILLING

10 g dried porcini mushrooms

150 g cream cheese

a handful of chives, snipped

sea salt and freshly ground black pepper

MAKES 16, SERVES 4–6

To make the filling, soak the dried porcini in boiling water for 20 minutes. Drain, squeeze dry and chop finely. Put in a bowl, add the cream cheese, chives, salt and pepper and mix well. Set aside.

Snap the stems off the mushrooms, then slice 5 mm off the flat side of each cap. Discard the trimmings. Mound 1–2 teaspoons of the filling into each mushroom and sandwich together to make 16 balls. Make sure the caps fit snugly together.

Mix the polenta or cornmeal, sesame seeds and salt in a bowl. Break the eggs into a small bowl and beat. Dip 1 ball into the egg, coat well, then roll in the polenta mixture, pressing the mixture onto any uncovered area. Repeat until all the balls have been used. Chill for 15 minutes or until needed.

Heat about 2 cm depth of oil in a large frying pan until hot or until a cube of bread browns in 30 seconds. Add the balls and fry for about 10 minutes until lightly golden all over. Remove with a slotted spoon and drain on crumpled kitchen paper. Serve hot.

large flour tortillas, 20 cm diameter

Cheddar cheese, grated, feta cheese, crumbled, or cream cheese

sunflower oil, for greasing

FILLING, CHOOSE FROM:

chopped tomatoes

chopped spring onions

chopped red chillies

sliced pickled jalapeño chillies

sliced pickled onions

finely sliced courgettes

sliced mushrooms

chopped peppers

chopped avocado

pitted black olives

mashed, canned refried beans, black beans, pinto beans or borlotti beans

ground cumin

pimentón (smoked paprika)

TO SERVE (OPTIONAL)

chopped coriander

plain yoghurt, crème fraîche or sour cream

SERVE 1 TORTILLA PER PERSON

Lightly grease a large frying pan with 1 teaspoon of oil. Lay a tortilla flat in the pan and cover with cheese and 4 or 5 fillings of your choice. Top with a second tortilla and press down gently. Cook over a moderate heat until the bottom tortilla is golden and crisp, about 5–7 minutes. Cover with a plate, turn the pan over and lift it off. Slide the inverted quesadilla back into the pan and cook as before. Cut into triangles.

Serve the quesadillas with chopped coriander and yoghurt, crème fraîche or sour cream, if using.

VARIATION

To grill or bake, put a tortilla on a lightly greased baking sheet, top with cheese, preferably Cheddar, and add 4 or 5 fillings of your choice. Cook under a hot grill or in a preheated oven at 180°C (350°F) Gas 4 for 10 minutes or until the cheese is golden.

quesadillas

You're heading for the fridge in search of something to demolish your small but acute appetite. You find some tomatoes, spring onions, cheese and a packet of flour tortillas – and hey presto! Your hunger will be zapped in less than 15 minutes. I haven't given quantities – there's no need, just pile on as much filling as you like. Fried, grilled or baked, this Mexican snack also makes excellent party food.

topped bruschetta

Bruschetta is a fancy Italian name for toast. But I'm not talking about any old toasted bread – it has to be a crusty, open-textured loaf, such as ciabatta, sourdough or country-style, rubbed with garlic and drizzled with olive oil. Pile high with either of these juicy toppings and serve 2 pieces per person for a stunning starter or 3 for a snack or light lunch.

1 ciabatta loaf or other country-style bread

1 fat garlic clove, halved crossways

fruity extra virgin olive oil, for drizzling

SLOW-ROASTED TOMATOES

1 kg plum or vine tomatoes, about 10

3 garlic cloves, sliced

2 tablespoons olive oil

2 teaspoons balsamic vinegar

a pinch of sugar

sea salt and freshly ground black pepper

5–6 basil leaves, torn, to serve (optional)

WILD MUSHROOMS WITH APPLES AND MADEIRA

1 tablespoon butter

200 g mixed wild mushrooms, such as chanterelles, ceps and oysters, or a mixture of wild and cultivated mushrooms, such as buttons and chestnuts, cleaned and sliced if large

1 Granny Smith apple, sliced

1 tablespoon freshly squeezed lemon juice

80 ml Madeira wine or dry sherry

75 g mascarpone cheese

sea salt and freshly ground black pepper

chopped parsley, to serve

SERVES 4–6.

To make the bruschetta, cut the bread into slices 2 cm thick. Rub the slices all over, especially the crust, with the cut end of the garlic halves and drizzle with olive oil. Toast or char-grill until golden and toasted on both sides.

To make the tomato topping, cut the plum tomatoes in half lengthways or the vine tomatoes in half crossways and put, cut side up, on a baking sheet lined with foil. Tuck in the garlic and drizzle with the olive oil and balsamic vinegar. Sprinkle with the sugar, salt and pepper, then roast in a preheated oven at 150°C (300°F) Gas 2 for 1½–2 hours, until the tomatoes have shrunken slightly and are golden at the edges. To serve, spoon onto the bruschetta and top with basil, if using.

To make the mushroom topping, melt the butter in a frying pan, add the mushrooms, salt and pepper and cook until softened. Toss the apple slices in the lemon juice, then add to the pan and sauté for 2–3 minutes. Add the Madeira or sherry and cook, stirring, until the alcohol has evaporated and the sauce has reduced slightly. Stir in the mascarpone until blended. To serve, spoon onto the bruschetta and sprinkle with chopped parsley.

spiced roasted nuts

Liven up a tossed salad or serve as party nibbles with drinks. I'm a great fan of nuts and seeds – my favourites being pumpkin seeds, which puff up impressively when roasted. Rich in iron and minerals, they are good for you, too. Mix your own selection of nuts – choose from sunflower seeds, pine nuts, cashews, macadamia nuts, pecans, Brazil nuts and almonds.

1 tablespoon olive oil

2 teaspoons dark soy sauce

a squeeze of fresh lemon juice

a pinch of sugar

3–4 drops Tabasco sauce

½ teaspoon paprika

1 teaspoon sesame seeds

150 g mixed raw nuts and/or seeds

MAKES 100 G

Put all the ingredients, except the nuts and/or seeds, in a bowl and whisk until mixed. Add the nuts and/or seeds, stir until coated, then tip onto a baking sheet and spread out in a single layer. Roast in a preheated oven at 190°C (375°F) Gas 5, stirring every 2 minutes, until golden and aromatic.

Let cool, then serve or store in an airtight container until needed.

25 g butter

4 shallots or 1 onion, sliced

100 g Cheddar or Gruyère cheese, grated

75 ml ale or lager

a pinch of sea salt

1 teaspoon mustard

2 eggs, lightly beaten

4 slices of bread

freshly ground black pepper

SERVES 2–4

rarebit

'Welsh rabbit' – also known as rarebit – is a glorified version of cheese on toast. It dates back to the mid-sixteenth century, but over time has evolved into countless variations. If you fancy a comforting snack or something light for brunch, lunch or supper, this easy-to-make rarebit is hard to beat.

Melt the butter in a heavy-based saucepan, add the shallots or onion and cook until softened. Add the cheese, ale or lager, mustard and salt. Stir over a low heat until the cheese has melted. Add the beaten eggs and stir until the mixture has thickened slightly, about 2–3 minutes. Don't overcook or you will end up with scrambled eggs. Toast the bread on both sides, then spoon the cheese mixture onto the toast and cook under a hot grill, until puffed and gold-flecked. Serve with lots of black pepper.

SWEET CHILLI SAUCE A great dipping sauce, especially good with wontons (page 114). Put 75 ml golden syrup, 1 tablespoon soy sauce and 1 tablespoon rice or cider vinegar in a bowl. Add 1 sliced red chilli and mix well. **MAKES 100 ML**

CHILLI COCONUT SAUCE For dipping or dressing stir-fried vegetables. Put 75 ml coconut cream, 2 teaspoons chilli paste and 2 teaspoons freshly squeezed lime juice in a bowl and mix well. **MAKES 100 ML**

ASIAN VINAIGRETTE Perfect for noodle salads. Put 1 tablespoon dark soy sauce, 1 tablespoon sesame oil and 1 tablespoon balsamic vinegar in a bowl and mix well. **MAKES 3 TABLESPOONS**

SOY-MAYO DRESSING Divine with potatoes or steamed vegetables. Put 75 ml good-quality mayonnaise in a bowl, add 2 tablespoons dark soy sauce and mix well. **MAKES 100 ML**

BLUE CHEESE DRESSING I A thick, creamy dressing for leafy salads. Mash 150 g Gorgonzola or dolcelatte cheese in a bowl. Add 3 tablespoons white wine vinegar, 125 ml olive oil and salt and pepper. Whisk until creamy and smooth. **MAKES 250 ML**

BLUE CHEESE DRESSING II Superb with Parmesan Patties (page 104) or baked potatoes. Put 100 g dolcelatte or Danish Blue and 100 g cottage cheese in a bowl. Mash with a fork until blended. **MAKES 200 G**

super-quick dressings and sauces

Strong flavours will liven up any dish – from raw or steamed vegetables to salads and barbecued food. You can also serve a selection of these high-speed accompaniments as dips at drinks parties.

dips, salsas & sauces

baba ganouj

A Middle Eastern aubergine purée. Charring the aubergines over an open flame gives them a subtle smoked flavour. You can also do this on a barbecue or in a super-hot oven. If you are oven-roasting, halve the aubergines lengthways, then score the flesh with a knife, drizzle with olive oil and roast at 220°C (425°F) Gas 7 until golden and softened. Peel, then follow the method in the recipe – gorgeous.

2 medium aubergines

juice of 1 lemon

1 garlic clove

2 tablespoons olive oil

2–3 tablespoons Greek or thick plain yoghurt

sea salt and freshly ground black pepper

MAKES ABOUT 500 ML

Push a fork into the stem-end of each aubergine and lay them directly over a high gas flame. Rotate the aubergines as the skin chars and blackens and continue to roast until softened, about 15 minutes. Steam will escape when cooked.

Transfer to a plate and let cool. Peel and discard the skin. Don't worry if a few charred bits remain – this will add extra flavour. Put the peeled flesh in a food processor, add the lemon juice, garlic, olive oil and yoghurt and blend to a purée. Add salt and pepper to taste. Alternatively, crush the garlic and put in a bowl with the peeled aubergines and other ingredients. Mash with a fork until smooth. Check the consistency: if you want a thinner dipping sauce, add more yoghurt or oil, as necessary. The texture of the dip will be coarser made this way than by machine.

Serve with toasted pita bread cut into triangles and raw vegetables, such as radishes, carrots, celery and mangetout.

sesame yoghurt dip

50 g sesame seeds

125 ml Greek or thick plain yoghurt

125 ml mayonnaise

2–3 tablespoons dark soy sauce

MAKES ABOUT 300 ML

Crudités will disappear in no time at all if you serve them with this dip. Use also as a sauce for steamed vegetables or a nutty dressing for salads. For a well-balanced flavour, I like to use half yoghurt and half mayonnaise, but you can use all mayonnaise or all yoghurt, if you prefer.

Put the sesame seeds in a dry frying pan and toast, stirring until lightly browned and beginning to jump around in the pan. Transfer to a bowl and let cool.

Add the yoghurt, mayonnaise and soy sauce and mix well. This dip is best eaten on the day it's made: otherwise the sesame seeds will lose their crunch.

This piquant mixture is a robust accompaniment for Breakfast Burrito (page 24), Haloumi Fajitas (page 82) and Tamales (page 84–6). It's also a splendid party dip. For barbecued food, try the corn or mango variation – its sweetness complements the smoky, charred flavours of outdoor cooking.

salsa fresca

Mix all the ingredients in a bowl and set aside for about 30 minutes for the flavours to develop.

MANGO SALSA

Replace the tomatoes with 300 g peeled and diced fresh mango. Use chopped mint instead of the coriander.

CORN SALSA

Instead of tomatoes, use 300 g corn kernels, fresh or frozen, then cooked in boiling water until tender. Alternatively, use canned corn, rinsed and drained.

300 g ripe tomatoes, finely chopped

1 small red onion, finely chopped

2 green chillies, deseeded and finely chopped

juice of 2–3 limes

a small handful of coriander, finely chopped

sea salt

MAKES 350 ML

pickled jalapeño salsa

OK, so the tomatoes come out of a can and the chillies out of a jar, but this salsa tastes sensationally authentic and has the added benefit of staying fresh and full of flavour for at least a couple of days in the refrigerator.

400 g canned chopped plum tomatoes

4 tablespoons sliced jalapeño peppers in vinegar, drained and coarsely chopped

2 tablespoons jalapeño vinegar from the jar

1 small onion, finely chopped

a handful of coriander, chopped

sea salt

MAKES 500 ML

Drain the tomatoes through a sieve, shaking to remove excess liquid, then discard the juice. Transfer the tomatoes to a bowl, add the remaining ingredients and stir to mix. Set aside for 30 minutes for the flavours to develop, then serve.

thyme and mushroom gravy

Gravy is usually served with traditional 'bangers and mash' – sausages and mashed potatoes. Vegetarians don't have to miss out on this classic dish as there are now many top-quality alternatives to meat sausages. Grill spicy, organic vegetarian sausages, then pile onto a bed of creamy mashed potatoes and top with gravy. Chase it all down with a glass of chilled beer.

2 tablespoons olive oil

1 onion, sliced

2 teaspoons fresh thyme leaves

1 bay leaf

50 g mushrooms, coarsely chopped

2 tablespoons plain flour

125 ml port or other fortified wine

250 ml vegetable stock

2 tablespoons dark soy sauce

SERVES 4

Heat the oil in a saucepan, add the onion and fry until golden. Add the herbs and mushrooms and cook until softened, about 5 minutes. Sprinkle with the flour and cook, stirring, for about 2 minutes. Stir in the port or wine, vegetable stock and soy sauce and simmer, stirring, until the gravy has thickened slightly, 3–5 minutes. Remove and discard the bay leaf. Pour the gravy into a jug and serve.

100 g dried butter beans, or 400 g canned butter beans

2 large heads of chicory (Belgian endive or witloof), about 500 g

50 g butter

4 leeks, about 350 g, sliced into 1 cm pieces

250 ml vegetable stock

250 ml port

2 tablespoons soy sauce

2 teaspoons sugar

4 sprigs of rosemary

1 bay leaf

1 small red chilli, deseeded and chopped, or ½ teaspoon dried chilli flakes

sea salt and freshly ground black pepper

SMOKED CHEESE MASH

1 kg floury potatoes, cut into equal-sized pieces

25 g butter

125 ml milk

200 g naturally smoked cheese, cut into cubes

sea salt

SERVES 4–6

If using dried butter beans, soak them overnight in cold water, then rinse and drain. Put in a saucepan, cover with water and bring to the boil. Cook for 10 minutes, then add salt and simmer for 30 minutes or until tender. Drain. If using canned beans, rinse and drain.

Cut the chicory lengthways into quarters, but do not trim off the base. Melt the butter in a large frying pan, add the chicory and cook, turning occasionally, until golden, about 10 minutes. Add the remaining ingredients, tucking in the rosemary and bay leaf. Bring to the boil, cover and simmer for 15 minutes. Turn the chicory over, increase the heat and cook for a further 10 minutes, until the leeks are tender and the gravy has thickened.

Meanwhile, cook the potatoes in salted boiling water for about 20 minutes, until tender. Drain thoroughly and return to the pan and set it over a low heat for 1 minute to steam dry. Add the butter and milk and mash until smooth. Stir in the smoked cheese, let stand for 2 minutes, then add salt to taste.

Spoon the potatoes onto warmed plates, top with the braised chicory and bean mixture and serve with the sauce poured over.

braised chicory and beans

with smoked cheese mash

Chicory – also known as Belgian endive – has a bitterness which some people find unpleasant, but others find addictive. Cooking helps reduce this taste and the flavour is balanced with the slight sweetness of the beans and aromatic gravy. Creamy mashed potatoes make this hearty meal complete.

main courses

roasted teriyaki tofu steaks

with glazed green vegetables

Dark soy sauce, sweet mirin and dry sake make up the unique flavours of teriyaki. Add fresh or dried shiitake mushrooms to the marinade for a richer flavour. Marinating the tofu in this assertive Japanese sauce also gives it a succulent, delicate character. You can buy ready-made teriyaki sauce, but it only faintly resembles the real thing, so try to make your own – it's very easy and well worth it.

500 g fresh firm tofu, cut into 4 pieces

4 fresh or dried shiitake mushrooms (optional)

200 g fresh or dried egg noodles

TERIYAKI MARINADE

125 ml dark soy sauce

125 ml mirin (Japanese sweet rice wine)

125 ml sake

1 tablespoon sugar

GLAZED GREEN VEGETABLES

2 tablespoons sunflower oil

2 garlic cloves, finely sliced

200 g broccoli florets or young purple sprouting broccoli, chopped

1 leek, white and light green parts finely sliced

200 g bok choy, quartered lengthways, or spinach, chopped

1 fennel bulb, trimmed and finely sliced

2 teaspoons cornflour mixed with 4 tablespoons cold water

TO SERVE

2 spring onions, finely sliced diagonally

1 tablespoon sesame seeds, pan-toasted

SERVES 4

To make the marinade, put the soy sauce, mirin, sake and sugar in a large frying pan and heat, stirring until the sugar has dissolved. Add the tofu and mushrooms, if using. Simmer gently for about 15 minutes, turning the tofu over halfway through cooking.

Transfer the tofu steaks to a lightly oiled baking dish or roasting tin. Spoon a little sauce on top and roast in a preheated oven at 220°C (425°F) Gas 7 for 10 minutes. Keep them warm. Using a slotted spoon, remove the mushrooms from the remaining sauce, squeeze dry and slice finely. Reserve the sauce.

To make the glazed vegetables, heat a wok until hot, then add the oil. Add the garlic, broccoli, leek and sliced mushrooms and stir-fry for 2 minutes. Add the bok choy or spinach and fennel. Stir-fry for 2 minutes. Add the reserved sauce and 75 ml water, stir, cover and cook for 2 minutes. Push the vegetables to the back of the wok, add the cornflour mixture to the bubbling juices and stir until thickened. Mix the vegetables into the sauce. Cook the noodles according to the packet instructions, then drain.

To serve, put a nest of noodles on warmed plates and pile on the vegetables. Turn the tofu steaks over and put shiny side up on top of the vegetables. Sprinkle with spring onions and toasted sesame seeds and serve.

piedmontese peppers

with gorgonzola polenta

Elizabeth David first popularized Piedmontese peppers in her book *Italian Food* in 1954. There is simply no better way of stuffing peppers. Olives and capers replace the traditional anchovies, adding a slight piquancy, while sweet tomatoes and basil caramelize slowly in rich garlicky juices.

The hollowed-out peppers make an excellent container for the filling, acting like a miniature roasting tin. Serve hot, warm or cold with grilled blue cheese polenta and rocket salad.

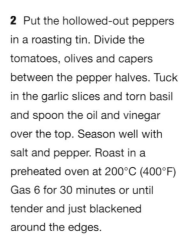

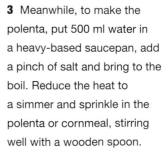

PIEDMONTESE PEPPERS

2 red peppers

2 ripe plum tomatoes, cut into quarters

8 black olives, pitted

1 tablespoon capers

2 garlic cloves, sliced

8 basil leaves, torn

4 tablespoons olive oil

2 teaspoons balsamic vinegar

sea salt and freshly ground black pepper

GORGONZOLA POLENTA

100 g polenta or coarse cornmeal

25 g butter

50 g Gorgonzola cheese, cut into small chunks

sea salt (optional)

TO SERVE

rocket leaves

SERVES 2–4

1 Cut each pepper in half lengthways. Do not remove the stems as this will help to keep the peppers' shape. Cut out the seeds and discard.

2 Put the hollowed-out peppers in a roasting tin. Divide the tomatoes, olives and capers between the pepper halves. Tuck in the garlic slices and torn basil and spoon the oil and vinegar over the top. Season well with salt and pepper. Roast in a preheated oven at 200°C (400°F) Gas 6 for 30 minutes or until tender and just blackened around the edges.

3 Meanwhile, to make the polenta, put 500 ml water in a heavy-based saucepan, add a pinch of salt and bring to the boil. Reduce the heat to a simmer and sprinkle in the polenta or cornmeal, stirring well with a wooden spoon.

4 Cook, stirring, until the mixture begins to pull away from the sides of the pan, about 15–30 minutes (depending on the quality and type of polenta) or according to the packet instructions. The polenta should be thick and lump-free.

5 Add the butter and salt, if needed, and stir well. (Do not overseason the polenta – the cheese is quite salty already.) Add the Gorgonzola and mix thoroughly.

6 Transfer to a shallow tray or wooden board (dampened with water to prevent sticking) and spread into a 21 cm square. Let cool until firm. The polenta can be made several hours ahead or the day before, then cooled and refrigerated until needed.

7 Cut the polenta into 4 squares, put on a non-stick baking sheet and cook under a very hot grill until the cheese begins to bubble and melt. To serve, transfer the polenta to warmed plates, top with the peppers and serve with rocket.

Pad Thai, probably the best-known of all Thai noodle dishes, takes only 5 minutes to cook. Use thick ribbon-like rice noodles ('rice sticks') for authenticity, or rice vermicelli or egg noodles. Tamarind, commonly used in Asian cooking, has a unique sour flavour, but you can substitute freshly squeezed lime juice.

pad thai noodles

Heat a wok until very hot, then add the oil. Add the eggs and noodles and stir-fry for about 2 minutes, until the eggs are lightly scrambled. Add the remaining ingredients and stir-fry for a further 3–5 minutes, until the noodles are cooked. Divide between 4 warmed bowls and serve sprinkled with the peanuts, spring onions and coriander.

4 tablespoons sunflower oil

4 eggs, lightly beaten

150 g dried thick rice noodles, soaked in warm water for 5 minutes, then drained

100 g kale or other leafy green, tough central core removed and leaves coarsely chopped

4 tablespoons tamarind paste or 2 tablespoons freshly squeezed lime juice

4 tablespoons sweet chilli sauce

4 tablespoons light soy sauce

1 large carrot, about 200 g, grated

100 g bean sprouts

TO SERVE

50 g roasted peanuts, chopped

4 spring onions, finely sliced

coriander leaves

SERVES 4

To make the spice paste, dry-toast the spice seeds in a frying pan, shaking until they pop and turn lightly golden. Transfer to a blender or spice grinder, add the remaining ingredients and 6 tablespoons water and grind to a smooth paste. Set aside.

Roast the aubergine directly over a high gas flame until charred and softened, about 15 minutes. Alternatively, roast in a preheated oven at 220°C (425°F) Gas 7 for about 40 minutes. Let cool, then peel and discard the skin. Don't worry if a few charred bits remain – this will add extra flavour.

Heat the oil or ghee in a large, heavy-based saucepan, add the onion and cook until softened. Add the spice paste and stir for 2 minutes to release the aromas, then add the pepper, sweet potatoes or yams, courgettes and chickpeas. Cover and cook, stirring occasionally, for 10 minutes. Add the tomatoes and 250 ml water, then bring to the boil and simmer, uncovered, for about 20 minutes.

Put the peeled aubergine in a blender, add the coconut milk and pulse to a coarse purée. Add to the pan and bring back to a simmer. Add salt, if necessary. Cook for 10 minutes, then remove from the heat, cover and let stand for at least 30 minutes or preferably overnight.

Reheat, then serve with rice, coriander sprigs, yoghurt and mango chutney.

charred aubergine and coconut curry

I wanted to re-create the subtle smoked flavour of Indian dishes cooked in a tandoor oven – and here is the result. Based on a charred, then puréed aubergine, this unusual curry is incredibly good. Don't be put off by the long list of ingredients for the spice paste – it's easy to make and will add a greater depth of flavour. The curry can be made in advance and, in fact, improves by being left overnight so that all the spicy flavours can develop.

1 medium aubergine, about 250 g

2 tablespoons vegetable oil or ghee

1 red onion, chopped

1 red pepper, chopped

250 g sweet potatoes or yams, peeled and cut into cubes

1 medium courgette, about 200 g

400 g canned chickpeas, rinsed and drained

400 g canned chopped tomatoes

250 ml unsweetened coconut milk

sea salt, to taste

SPICE PASTE

1 tablespoon cumin seeds

1 tablespoon coriander seeds

½ teaspoon cardamom seeds, about 10 pods

½ teaspoon fenugreek seeds

5 cm fresh ginger, peeled and grated

4 garlic cloves

1 teaspoon turmeric

1–2 chillies, deseeded, or 1 teaspoon dried chilli flakes

1 tomato, cut into quarters

2 teaspoons sea salt

1 teaspoon sugar

TO SERVE

steamed basmati rice

sprigs of coriander

mango chutney

thick plain yoghurt

SERVES 4–6

pumpkin and tofu laksa

Laksa is a Malaysian curry. It usually consists of rice noodles, crunchy raw vegetables and fragrant herbs, bathed in a spicy coconut soup. The distinctive perfume of fresh lemongrass and kaffir lime leaves is fundamental to the spice paste and these are available from Asian food stores and markets. If you can't find these aromatics, replace them with grated lime zest and fresh lemon juice, or use a store-bought laksa paste or Thai curry paste instead, but read the label carefully – most contain ground shrimp.

250 g peeled, deseeded
pumpkin or butternut squash,
cut into 1 cm cubes

300 g tofu, dried with kitchen
paper and cut into 4 triangles

200 g creamed coconut, chopped
and dissolved in
500 ml boiling water, or
800 ml coconut milk

4 tablespoons light soy sauce

2 teaspoons sugar

150 g rice vermicelli noodles

150 g beansprouts

1 medium tomato, cut into
8 wedges

5 cm cucumber, cut into
thin strips

8 sprigs of coriander

a large handful of mint leaves

2 spring onions, chopped

sunflower oil, for frying

SPICE PASTE

2 garlic cloves, coarsely chopped

2 red chillies, deseeded and
coarsely chopped

5 cm fresh ginger, peeled and
finely grated

1 small onion

¼ teaspoon ground turmeric

2 stalks lemongrass, sliced

4 kaffir lime leaves, chopped

SERVES 4

1 To make the spice paste, put all the ingredients and 3 tablespoons water in a blender or spice grinder and purée until smooth (add more water, if necessary).

2 Put the pumpkin or squash in a saucepan, then add salt and 500 ml water. Bring to the boil, then simmer for 10 minutes, until the cubes are tender, but still chunky. Drain, reserving the cooking liquid.

3 Heat 2 cm depth of sunflower oil in a wok or frying pan. Add the tofu and fry until golden and crisp all over. Remove with a slotted spoon and drain on crumpled kitchen paper. Set aside.

4 Heat 2 tablespoons of the oil in a saucepan, add the spice paste and fry for 2 minutes to release the aromas. Add the coconut liquid or coconut milk, fried tofu, soy sauce and sugar. Add the reserved pumpkin liquid. Bring to the boil, then simmer for 10 minutes.

5 Meanwhile, put the noodles in a bowl, cover with boiling water and let soak for 5 minutes. Drain and divide between 4 warmed bowls.

6 Top with the beansprouts, tomatoes and cooked pumpkin or squash. Add a piece of fried tofu to each bowl.

7 Ladle over the hot coconut soup, top with the cucumber, coriander, mint and spring onions, then serve.

Fajitas – usually made with beef or chicken – are utterly delicious and can be adapted easily for vegetarians, using haloumi. This firm cheese from Cyprus is unique; it won't melt when fried and develops a delicious crisp crust. Eat the fajitas as soon as you make them; the haloumi loses tenderness if left for too long after cooking. If you can't find this cheese, use tempeh (page 10), found in the frozen section in health food shops.

haloumi fajitas

To make the marinade, put the garlic and salt in a mortar and crush to a paste with a pestle. Transfer to a bowl, add the remaining ingredients, except the oil, and whisk together. Add the oil in a steady stream, whisking until the mixture has emulsified. Put the haloumi or tempeh in a shallow dish, add enough marinade to cover and turn until coated. Put the peppers, onions, courgettes and mushrooms in a bowl, add the remaining marinade and mix well. Cover both dishes and let marinate in the refrigerator for at least 30 minutes.

Stack the tortillas, wrap in foil and put in a preheated oven at 150°C (300°F) Gas 2 for about 15 minutes until warm. Meanwhile, heat a large frying pan or wok until very hot, add the marinated vegetables and liquid and stir-fry until the juices have evaporated and the vegetables are golden and slightly caramelized, about 20 minutes. Transfer to a heatproof dish, cover and keep it warm in the oven.

Drain the haloumi or tempeh, discarding the marinade. Put the slices in the pan or wok in a single layer. (If using tempeh, add 3 tablespoons olive oil to the pan.) Cook over a moderate heat for about 10 minutes, turning halfway through cooking, until golden.

Serve the tortillas, vegetables and cheese separately, so that people can make their own fajitas. To assemble, put a warm tortilla on a plate, add a spoonful of vegetables to one half and top with haloumi or tempeh. Bring the uncovered half of the tortilla up over the filling, then tuck the corners underneath the fajitas. Serve with guacamole, salsa and lots of sour cream, crème fraîche or yoghurt.

500 g haloumi cheese or tempeh, sliced

2 red onions, halved and cut into wedges

1 red pepper, deseeded and cut into strips

1 yellow pepper, deseeded and cut into strips

1 green pepper, deseeded and cut into strips

1 medium or 2 small courgettes, quartered lengthways and cut into chunks

200 g button mushrooms

MARINADE

2 garlic cloves

1 tablespoon coarse sea salt

4 limes, the grated zest of 2 and the juice of all

a handful of fresh coriander, chopped

½ teaspoon dried oregano

½ teaspoon dried chilli flakes

1 teaspoon cumin seeds

1 teaspoon sugar

1 tablespoon white wine vinegar

125 ml dark rum

125 ml olive oil

TO SERVE

8–10 large flour tortillas, 20 cm diameter

Guacamole (page 13)

Pickled Jalapeño Salsa or Salsa Fresca (pages 62–3)

sour cream, crème fraîche or thick plain yoghurt

SERVES 4–6

tamales

These simple cornmeal parcels originated in ancient Mexico and are often eaten at fiestas and family celebrations. Masa harina – a special type of ground maize – is used in the filling, then the tamales are wrapped in a corn-husk jacket before being gently steamed. (Banana leaves also make an excellent protective wrap.) The result – light, fluffy mounds. Blue masa harina is so called because the maize is actually this colour. It has the best corn flavour, but, if you can't find it, use polenta instead. Serve with rice, refried beans and salsa for a substantial main course.

100 g butter

175 g blue masa harina* or polenta

a pinch of sea salt

1 teaspoon baking powder

1 dried smoked chilli*, soaked in hot water for 20 minutes, then drained, deseeded and chopped (optional)

about 125 ml vegetable stock or water

175 g Cheddar cheese or Monterey Jack cheese, cut into 8 blocks, 1 cm x 6 cm

8–10 dried corn husks* or 2–3 banana leaves

TO SERVE

canned refried beans

steamed white rice

Salsa Fresca (page 63)

MAKES 8, SERVES 4

* Available from specialist Latin American food stores.

1 Put the butter in a food processor and mix until light and fluffy. Add the masa harina or polenta, salt, baking powder and chilli, if using, and mix. With the machine running, slowly pour in enough stock or water through the feed tube to make a soft dough.

2 Divide the corn dough into 8 pieces and mould each one around a block of cheese until completely enclosed.

3 If using dried corn husks, soak them in boiling water for several minutes until softened, then drain and separate the layers. Wrap the tamales in a layer of husk, covering with extra bits of husk, if necessary.

4 Using thin strips of husk, tie each end of the parcel close to the filling to look like a Christmas cracker. Repeat until all the tamales are wrapped and tied.

5 If using banana leaves, cut 16 strips, 6 cm wide. Put a tamale at the bottom of a strip and roll up. Wrap a second strip around the open ends to close.

6 Push a cocktail stick through the middle of the parcel to secure. Repeat wrapping in banana leaves and cooking until all the tamales are made.

7 Put the tamales in a bamboo steamer set over a saucepan of simmering water. Steam for 1 hour. Serve the refried beans, rice and salsa separately, so people can help themselves and unwrap their own tamales. This is the fun part!

To make the coulis, heat the olive oil in a saucepan, add the garlic and ginger and fry until fragrant. Add the tomatoes, vinegar, sugar and Madeira or sherry and simmer gently for 20–30 minutes, stirring frequently. Add salt and cayenne pepper to taste. Transfer to a blender and purée until smooth. For an extra-smooth consistency, strain the purée through a sieve. Set aside.

Put the trimmed spinach in a large saucepan, cover and heat, stirring occasionally, until just wilted. Drain and let cool. Wring out in a clean tea towel, then chop.

Heat the olive oil in the pan, add the onions, mushrooms, coriander and cinnamon, salt and pepper and cook until softened and the juices have evaporated. Add the garlic, fry briefly, then add the chestnuts. Cook for 1–2 minutes, then add the spinach and marmalade and heat through. Season to taste.

Working with 1 sheet of filo at a time (keep the rest covered with a damp cloth to stop them drying out), line the prepared tin. Press a sheet gently into the sides of the tin and let the edges overhang. Brush with melted butter and slightly overlap with another sheet. Continue to layer and butter the sheets as before, until the tin is completely covered. Spoon in the chestnut mixture and smooth flat. Fold the overhanging filo in towards the centre and ruffle the top so the filo stands in peaks. Brush with butter.

Bake in a preheated oven at 180°C (350°F) Gas 4 for 30 minutes, then unmould carefully and slide onto a baking sheet. Return to the oven for a further 20 minutes, until golden and crisp all over. Let stand for a few minutes. Reheat the coulis. Using a serrated knife, cut the torte into wedges and serve with the coulis poured over.

chestnut, spinach and mushroom filo torte

with tomato and ginger coulis

A star replacement for turkey at a vegetarian Christmas dinner or special meal – packed with fresh, spicy, rich flavours. The buttery filo is light and crisp, but use olive oil if you are cooking for vegans. Ready-cooked, vacuum-packed chestnuts are extremely convenient to use and the filling can be made a day in advance.

500 g spinach leaves, well washed, with tough stalks removed

2 tablespoons olive oil

2 onions, chopped

400 g mushrooms, chopped

2 teaspoons ground coriander

2 teaspoons ground cinnamon

3 garlic cloves, chopped

400 g cooked, peeled chestnuts, chopped

2 heaped tablespoons thick-cut marmalade

5 sheets filo pastry, about 28 x 48 cm

about 50 g butter, melted

sea salt and freshly ground black pepper

TOMATO AND GINGER COULIS

75 ml olive oil

4 garlic cloves, chopped

5 cm fresh ginger, peeled and chopped

800 g canned chopped tomatoes

1 tablespoon balsamic vinegar

1 tablespoon dark brown sugar

150 ml Madeira wine or dry sherry

sea salt and cayenne pepper

24 cm springform cake tin, brushed with melted butter

SERVES 6–8

1 medium courgette, about 250 g, cut lengthways into 5 mm slices

5 tablespoons olive oil

3 garlic cloves, chopped

400 g canned chopped plum tomatoes

½ teaspoon balsamic vinegar

1 teaspoon dark brown sugar

2 handfuls of basil, leaves torn or coarsely chopped

250 ml arborio risotto rice, measured by volume

100 g mozzarella cheese, cut into 1 cm cubes

100 g Fontina or other mature, hard cheese, cut into 5 mm cubes

50 g freshly grated Parmesan cheese

4 tablespoons toasted breadcrumbs

sea salt and freshly ground black pepper

450 g loaf tin, lightly oiled

SERVES 4–6

Heat a stove-top grill pan until very hot. Brush both sides of the courgette slices with 2 tablespoons of the oil. Add to the pan and sear, turning halfway through cooking, until softened and marked with black stripes. Alternatively, put on an oiled baking sheet, add salt and pepper and roast in a preheated oven at 200°C (400°F) Gas 6 for 15–20 minutes until golden.

Heat the remaining oil in a saucepan, add the garlic and fry until fragrant. Add the tomatoes, vinegar, sugar, salt and pepper. Simmer for 10 minutes or until the sauce has thickened slightly. Stir in the basil.

Add the rice to a saucepan of boiling salted water (there is no need to measure the water). Bring back to the boil, then reduce the heat and simmer until the rice is tender, but still firm (al dente), about 10 minutes. Drain.

Add the rice to the tomato sauce and mix well. Stir in the cheeses and add salt and pepper, if necessary.

Sprinkle 2 tablespoons of the breadcrumbs into the prepared loaf tin, tipping the tin from side to side until coated. Spoon in half the rice mixture and smooth flat. Add the courgettes in a single layer, then top with the remaining rice. Smooth flat, pressing down firmly. Sprinkle with the remaining breadcrumbs. (The torta may be refrigerated at this point, then cooked later.)

Bake in a preheated oven at 220°C (425°F) Gas 7 for 30–40 minutes or until golden and bubbling around the edges. Let stand for 10 minutes. Run a long-bladed, sharp knife between the torta and the tin, then turn out onto a board or platter, tap the tin all over and lift it off. Cut the torta into slices and serve with a green salad.

Listen to the 'oohs' and 'aahs' as you present this dish to hungry friends. It's a totally new way of serving risotto – and the secret vegetable layer is so unexpected. I particularly like courgettes but you can experiment with other vegetables: char-grilled aubergines, peppers or asparagus are all delicious. Give yourself a head start – make the torta up to a day in advance, chill until needed, then let it reach room temperature before baking.

torta di risotto
with char-grilled courgettes and three cheeses

Cut the aubergine lengthways into quarters and score the flesh with a crisscross pattern. Slice the courgettes in half lengthways. Cut a thin slice off the bottom of the onions and cut a cross in the top. Split the chillies in half. Leave the garlic whole.

Put all the vegetables, except the tomatoes, cut side up in a roasting tin or dish. Tuck the rosemary and chillies into the onions. Brush all but 2 tablespoons of oil all over the vegetables, then drizzle with the lemon juice and add salt and pepper.

Roast in a preheated oven at 200°C (400°F) Gas 6 for 30 minutes, then brush the tomatoes with the remaining oil and put on top of the half-roasted vegetables. Cook for 15–20 minutes until the vegetables are golden and the tomatoes have split. If using cherry tomatoes, add them after 40 minutes and roast for a further 5–10 minutes.

1 aubergine

2 courgettes

4 red onions, unpeeled

2 red chillies

1 whole head of garlic, unpeeled

4 tomatoes on the vine or 16 cherry tomatoes on the vine

4 sprigs of rosemary

10 tablespoons olive oil

juice of ½ lemon

coarse sea salt and freshly ground black pepper

SERVES 4

provençal roasted vegetables

Preparation is kept to a minimum and the result is a thing of beauty. Make sure you provide a side plate to put the bits on as people pluck their way through the sweet, juicy vegetables.

minted char-grilled courgettes

Perfect for a summer lunch, this Mediterranean recipe and simple char-grilling technique bring out the best in courgettes. They cook to a sensuous texture and absorb the contrasting flavours of the tangy vinegar and fragrant mint.

4 medium courgettes, about 1 kg

2 tablespoons olive oil

4 teaspoons white wine vinegar

a handful of mint, leaves torn

sea salt and freshly ground black pepper

SERVES 4

Trim and discard the ends off the courgettes, then cut the vegetable lengthways into ribbon-like slices and put in a bowl. Drizzle with the olive oil and, using your hands, gently toss the slices until well coated.

Heat a stove-top grill pan or non-stick frying pan until very hot. Add the courgette ribbons (in batches, if necessary) and cook until softened and marked with black stripes on both sides. Transfer to a shallow dish and drizzle with the vinegar while the courgettes are still warm. Add salt and pepper and let cool.

Pile the courgette ribbons into a serving bowl, sprinkle with the mint and add lots of freshly ground black pepper. Serve.

12 shallots, unpeeled

8 garlic cloves, unpeeled

1 kg orange-fleshed sweet potatoes, cut into even chunks

1 teaspoon coriander seeds, crushed

2 red chillies

6 tablespoons olive oil

sea salt and freshly ground black pepper

SERVES 4

Put the shallots and garlic in a bowl, cover with boiling water, let soak for 30 minutes, then drain and peel. The skins should slip off easily.

Transfer to a roasting tin and add the sweet potatoes, coriander seeds and whole chillies. Add the olive oil, salt and pepper and toss well to coat.

Roast in a preheated oven at 200°C (400°F) Gas 6 for 30 minutes until golden and tender. Shake the tin from time to time during cooking and brush the vegetables with the pan juices.

roasted sweet potatoes
with shallots, garlic and chillies

Crisp, golden and bravely flavoured is how I like my sweet potatoes. This recipe is for garlic and chilli lovers everywhere!

lemon-roasted baby potatoes

Potatoes love to be roasted. These zesty little spuds have a crisp tangy exterior and are fluffy inside. Serve with steamed greens or roasted vegetables.

1 kg baby new potatoes, scrubbed

4 tablespoons olive oil

2 lemons, grated zest of both and juice of 1

1 teaspoon sugar

sea salt and freshly ground black pepper

SERVES 4

Cook the potatoes in salted boiling water for 5 minutes, drain, then transfer to a roasting tin.

Whisk the olive oil, lemon zest and juice, sugar, salt and pepper in a bowl, pour over the potatoes and toss well to coat.

Roast in a preheated oven at 190°C (375°F) Gas 5 for 20–30 minutes, turning and basting frequently with the pan juices, until golden and tender.

chilli greens

with garlic crisps

I often have cravings for dark green vegetables – probably because they're rich in iron and vitamin C. The word 'greens' – used loosely to describe any leafy green – includes spring greens, Swiss chard, bok choy, beetroot leaves, spinach and much more. Many need only brief cooking – steam or stir-fry to retain colour, nutrients and flavour. Remove any tough stalks before cooking.

500 g greens (see introduction above)

2 tablespoons olive oil

4 garlic cloves, sliced

1 red chilli, deseeded and finely sliced

sea salt and freshly ground black pepper

SERVES 4

Coarsely chop the greens, but, if using bok choy, cut lengthways into wedges. Gently heat the olive oil in a large saucepan. Add the garlic, fry until golden and crisp, about 2–3 minutes, then remove and set aside. Add the chilli to the infused oil in the pan and cook for 1 minute. Tip in the greens – they will splutter, so stand back. Add salt and pepper and mix well. Cover and cook, turning the greens occasionally using tongs, until tender: spring greens, about 5 minutes; Swiss chard, bok choy and beetroot leaves, about 3 minutes; and spinach, about 1–2 minutes.

Transfer to a warmed serving dish and top with the garlic crisps.

VARIATION

For a festive treat, perfect at Christmas, omit the garlic and chilli. Fry 50 g pine nuts in the oil until golden, then remove and set aside. Add the greens, the grated zest of 1 orange and 1 teaspoon sugar and cook as described above. Serve with the pine nuts and 75 g redcurrants sprinkled on top.

Turn ordinary vegetables into something fabulous with this gorgeous Thai-flavoured sauce. Use it as a marinade here, but also try it as a ketchup – on veggie burgers or on the vegetarian version of a hot dog. The sauce will keep for a week in the fridge.

thai-glazed vegetable skewers

To make the sauce, put the creamed coconut in a bowl, add 3 tablespoons boiling water and dissolve to make a thick paste. Transfer to a blender or food processor, add the remaining ingredients and blend until smooth.

Peel the mango with a sharp knife and stand it upright on a board, narrow end pointing up. Slice off thick cheeks parallel to the stone and cut off strips around the stone. Cut the flesh into equal chunks.

Thread the skewers with the fruit and vegetable chunks, each starting and ending with a lime leaf, if using. Brush the sauce generously over the loaded skewers, then cover and let marinate in the refrigerator for at least 30 minutes. Reserve the remaining sauce.

Put on a hot barbecue or stove-top grill pan or under a preheated grill and cook, turning occasionally and basting with the remaining sauce, until tender and lightly charred.

1 large, firm, ripe mango

1 yellow pepper, deseeded and cut into 10 pieces

2 small red onions, cut into 10 wedges

2 small courgettes, cut into 10 pieces

1–2 limes, cut into 10 slices

10 button mushrooms

1 red pepper, deseeded and cut into 10 pieces

5 chillies, halved (optional)

20 kaffir lime leaves (optional)

THAI BARBECUE SAUCE

50 g block creamed coconut, chopped

75 ml dark soy sauce

2 tablespoons soft brown sugar

2 tablespoons rice wine vinegar or freshly squeezed lime juice

3 tablespoons tomato purée

3 kaffir lime leaves, chopped

1 stalk lemongrass, finely sliced

1–2 bird's eye chillies, sliced

1 fat garlic clove, sliced

2 tablespoons sunflower oil

10 metal or long bamboo skewers (if bamboo, soak in water for 30 minutes)

MAKES 10

vegetarian barbecue

feta-stuffed peppers

The stuffing is not cooked, merely heated through and is more like a warm salad than a hot filling. Roasting the peppers on a barbecue gives them a unique, smoky flavour and their natural sweetness combines perfectly with the tangy wheat salad.

Put the bulghur wheat in a bowl, cover with boiling water and let stand for 30 minutes, until the grains are puffed and swollen. Drain, if necessary.

Cut the peppers in half lengthways and scrape out and discard the seeds and membranes. Leave the stalk, which will help hold the pepper in shape.

Put the remaining ingredients in a bowl, add the soaked bulghur, season with salt and pepper and mix well. Pile the stuffing into the pepper halves.

Cook on a hot barbecue or stove-top grill pan until the peppers are tender and blackened underneath and the stuffing is warmed through. Serve with a crisp, green salad and warmed pita bread.

100 g bulghur wheat

2 red, yellow or orange peppers

150 g feta cheese, crumbled

3 handfuls of mixed fresh herbs, such as parsley, mint, dill, basil and coriander, chopped

1 garlic clove, crushed

2 teaspoons finely grated fresh ginger

1 tablespoon sumac or 1 tablespoon freshly squeezed lemon juice

2 tablespoons olive oil

sea salt and freshly ground black pepper

SERVES 4

parmesan patties

Great outdoor food. Kids and grown-ups can't resist burgers and these are no exception. Make in advance to save time, then chill or freeze until needed. Oven-bake rather than barbecue for best results. Let's face it, you'll be popping in and out of the kitchen anyway, so these patties will leave space free on the barbecue for other things.

Heat the oil in a frying pan, add the onions, mushrooms, thyme and salt and fry until softened and golden. Let cool.

Transfer to a food processor, add the cheeses, beans, breadcrumbs and freshly ground pepper. Pulse until mixed, then add the soy sauce, wine, mustard, egg and cornflour. Process until mixed, but not too smooth.

Using wet hands, shape the mixture into 8 balls, then flatten into 2 cm thick patties. Put on the prepared baking sheet, cover with clingfilm and chill until firm. (At this point, you can freeze the patties, then cook from frozen when needed.)

When ready to cook, brush the tops with extra oil and bake in a preheated oven at 220°C (425°F) Gas 7 for 25 minutes, until golden and crisp (5–10 minutes longer if cooking from frozen).

Cut the rolls in half and toast or grill lightly on one side, add the patties and your choice of accompaniments, then close up and serve.

1 tablespoon olive oil, plus extra for brushing

2 medium onions, chopped

125 g mushrooms, coarsely chopped

1 teaspoon fresh thyme leaves

50 g Parmesan cheese, coarsely grated

50 g Cheddar cheese, grated

150 g canned borlotti or pinto beans, rinsed and drained

100 g fresh breadcrumbs

1 tablespoon soy sauce

2 tablespoons red wine

1 teaspoon mustard

1 egg, beaten

1 tablespoon cornflour

8 soft bread rolls

sea salt and freshly ground black pepper

TO SERVE (OPTIONAL)

salad leaves or rocket

sliced tomatoes

sliced red onions

tomato ketchup

mayonnaise

chilli sauce

Blue Cheese Dressing II (see page 59)

MAKES ABOUT 8 PATTIES

turkish stuffed aubergines

If one vegetable could sum up Turkish cooking, it would be the aubergine. I discovered this very clever idea for stuffing whole aubergines in a Turkish cookbook and not only is the process ingenious, but it is also great fun. Use long, slender aubergines, which are perfect for hollowing out and stuffing in this way: the plump variety may take too long to cook evenly without burning. Turn the aubergines often on the barbecue until they are tender and the skin is deeply browned all over.

2 medium aubergines,
preferably long and thin

100 g couscous

3 tablespoons olive oil, plus
extra for brushing

2 medium onions, chopped

4 garlic cloves, chopped

1 teaspoon ground cinnamon

1 teaspoon cumin seeds

50 g pine nuts

6 dates, pitted and chopped

1 tablespoon orange flower
water (optional)

a handful of flat leaf parsley,
chopped

1 medium tomato, cut in half

sea salt and freshly ground
black pepper

TO SERVE

Greek or thick plain yoghurt

lemon wedges

SERVES 4

1 Using a rolling pin, gently beat the aubergines all over without breaking the skin. Massage, rolling them back and forth on a work surface until collapsed and quite flat, about 2 cm thick.

2 Make a shallow cut around the stem-end of the aubergines, but do not cut through completely. Twist the top, then pull it off; the core should come away too. Scoop out the inside of the aubergines and coarsely chop. Set aside. Sprinkle a little salt inside the cavity, then put the aubergines, cut side down, in a colander over a bowl to drain.

3 To make the filling, put the couscous in a bowl, cover with boiling water and let soak for 15 minutes. Drain if necessary. Fluff the grains with a fork, then set aside. Heat 2 tablespoons of the olive oil in a frying pan, add the onions, chopped aubergines and salt and fry until softened and golden. Add the garlic, cinnamon and cumin and cook for 2 minutes, until fragrant.

4 Transfer to a bowl. Heat the remaining oil in the pan and add the pine nuts. Fry until golden, then add to the mixture, along with the dates, orange flower water, if using, parsley and couscous. Season with salt and pepper and mix well.

5 Spoon the mixture into the aubergines, pushing it firmly into the cavities (the aubergines should resume their former shape).

6 Push half a tomato into the top of each stuffed aubergine to plug the hole. Brush lightly all over with olive oil.

7 Cook on a hot barbecue, turning frequently, until very tender and well browned, about 30 minutes. Slice into thick discs and serve with yoghurt and lemon wedges.

NOTE : To cook in the oven, put the aubergines in a roasting tin and pour in 1 cm depth vegetable stock and 2 tablespoons olive oil. Cover with foil and roast in a preheated oven at 200°C (400°F) Gas 6 for 30–40 minutes, until very tender.

These barbecued mushrooms are so juicy and have a sensational texture. Use tomatoes, mozzarella and onions that are the same diameter as the mushrooms so they fit snugly into the caps. A luxurious splash of truffle oil intensifies the earthy mushroom flavour.

stuffed flat mushrooms
with mozzarella and truffle oil

4 large, open-cap field mushrooms

olive oil, for brushing

4 teaspoons truffle oil

4 thin onion slices, the same diameter as the mushrooms

1 mozzarella, about 150 g, cut into 4 slices

a handful of basil leaves, 4 whole, the rest finely sliced

4 large tomato slices, the same diameter as the mushrooms

sea salt and freshly ground black pepper

SERVES 4

Cut the stalks out of the mushrooms and discard. Brush the caps with olive oil and put, gill-side up, on a plate or tray. Season with salt and pepper and drizzle the truffle oil onto the gills.

Put a slice of onion inside the cavity of each mushroom, then layer with a slice of mozzarella, a leaf of basil and a slice of tomato. Season with salt and pepper, sprinkle with the finely sliced basil and drizzle with olive oil.

Cook on a hot barbecue for about 15 minutes (without turning), until the mushrooms have softened and shrunk slightly and the cheese has melted. Serve with ciabatta bread.

mushroom and onion marmalade tartlets

A cross between a tartlet and an open sandwich. These no-fuss party tartlets are so simple to make – there's not even any pastry to make or roll out. It doesn't matter how many tartlets I make, there never seems to be enough to go round – everyone keeps coming back for more. Serve hot for best results.

2 tablespoons olive oil

1 large onion, chopped

250 g mushrooms, finely chopped or sliced

1 tablespoon sugar

leaves from 2–3 sprigs of thyme

12 slices medium-sliced white bread

unsalted butter, for spreading

250 g Gruyère or mature Cheddar cheese, grated

sea salt and freshly ground black pepper

a 6-cm glass or plain biscuit cutter

two non-stick, 12-hole bun tins or shallow muffin tins

MAKES 24

Heat the olive oil in a frying pan, add the onions and fry until softened and lightly golden. Sprinkle the sugar on top and season with salt and pepper. Add the mushrooms and thyme and cook over a high heat until the mushrooms have softened, about 5 minutes.

Using the top of the glass or biscuit cutter, stamp out circles from the bread. (The glass flattens the bread at the edges, which will make the tartlets crisper.) Lightly spread butter on one side of each circle, then use to line the tin, butter side down, and press firmly into place.

Put teaspoonfuls of the mushroom mixture in the bread cups and top with the grated cheese. Bake in a preheated oven at 220°C (425°F) Gas 7 for about 10–15 minutes until golden and bubbling. Serve hot. Alternatively, let cool, then warm through before serving.

party food

spinach and water chestnut wontons

Fried nibbles are always a favourite at parties. These crisp, golden pockets with a light filling, dipped in a sweet, fiery sauce, will be devoured in moments. Wonton wrappers come in two sizes: 8 cm or 10 cm squares, available fresh or frozen from Asian supermarkets. For this recipe, you will need the small ones. As with all fried foods, wontons are best served as soon as they are cooked and do not reheat successfully. However, you can prepare them in advance, cover and cook at the last minute – they'll be a huge hit.

250 g spinach leaves, tough stalks removed

6 canned water chestnuts, drained and finely chopped

2 teaspoons finely grated fresh ginger

a pinch of sea salt

20 small wonton wrappers*

1 egg, beaten

cornflour, for dusting

sunflower oil, for frying

TO SERVE

Sweet Chilli Sauce (page 59)

MAKES 20

* Packets of wonton wrappers are available two sizes; 10 cm large with about 40 wrappers, or 8 cm small with about 70 wrappers. Leftover wrappers may be frozen.

1 Put the spinach in a large saucepan, cover and heat, stirring occasionally until just wilted. Drain, pressing out excess moisture. Let cool, then wring out in a clean tea towel until dry. Chop finely, put in a bowl, add the water chestnuts, ginger and salt and mix.

2 Take the wonton wrappers out of the plastic bag, but keep them covered as you work to prevent them drying out. Put a wrapper on the work surface, brush the edges with egg and put about 1–2 teaspoons of the spinach mixture in the middle.

3 To shape the wonton, fold in half (with the filling inside) to make a triangle. Press to seal.

4 Bend the wonton into a crescent shape and bring the 2 opposite longest points together. Stick with a little egg. Repeat, filling and shaping until all the spinach mixture has been used. Refrigerate or freeze any remaining wrappers.

5 Transfer the wontons to a plate dusted with cornflour, turn gently until lightly coated, then shake off any excess cornflour. (This stops the wontons sticking together).

6 Fill a wok or large saucepan one-third full of oil and heat to 190°C (375°F). To test, drop in a piece of wonton wrapper – it will puff up immediately when the oil is at the right temperature. Add the wontons in batches of 5–6 and cook for 1–2 minutes, turning once, until puffed and golden.

7 Remove with a slotted spoon or large straining spoon and drain on crumpled kitchen paper. Serve hot with Sweet Chilli Sauce for dipping.

mozzarella and cherry tomato skewers

A classic mix of Italian colours and flavours – in miniature. Bocconcini (meaning 'little bites') are tiny balls of mozzarella. They're perfect for these skewers, but, if you can't find them, use regular mozzarella instead and cut it into 20 cubes. Choose the best olives you can find – marinated if possible.

10 cherry tomatoes, halved

20 basil leaves

10 bocconcini balls, halved, or 150 g regular mozzarella, cubed

20 black olives, pitted

olive oil for drizzling

sea salt and freshly ground black pepper

20 cocktail sticks

MAKES 20

Thread the tomato halves, basil leaves, bocconcini or mozzarella cubes and olives onto the cocktail sticks. Lightly drizzle olive oil over the loaded skewers and season with salt and lots of black pepper. Serve.

feta and cumin filo parcels

3 sheets filo pastry, about 28 x 48 cm

50 g unsalted butter, melted

FILLING

1 tablespoon cumin seeds

150 g feta cheese, finely crumbled

a handful of mint leaves, finely chopped

finely grated zest of 1 lemon

baking sheet, lightly greased

MAKES 24

Flaky, bite-size parcels are quick and simple to make. Feta cheese is quite salty, so you won't need additional seasoning in these savouries – only lots of cool drinks to quench your thirst. Serve Chilli Coconut Sauce (page 59) for dipping.

To make the filling, dry-toast the cumin seeds in a frying pan until fragrant and lightly golden. Put in a bowl, add the feta, mint and lemon zest and mix well.

Put 1 sheet of pastry on a work surface (keep the rest covered with a damp cloth to stop them drying out) and brush with a little melted butter. Lay a second sheet on top and brush with more butter. Repeat with the final sheet.

Cut into 24 squares, about 7.5 cm. Put 1 teaspoon of the filling in the middle of each square, then bring the 4 corners to the centre and press along the seams to seal. Dab with melted butter and cover with clingfilm until ready to bake.

Put the filo parcels on the prepared baking sheet and bake in a preheated oven at 200°C (400°F) Gas 6 for about 10 minutes, until golden. Serve warm or cold.

5 quails' eggs

2 small heads of chicory
(Belgian endive or
witloof)

50 g bean sprouts

¼ red pepper, finely
sliced lengthways into
5 cm strips

50 g red cabbage, finely
sliced

1 spring onion, finely
sliced lengthways
into 5 cm strips

5 cm cucumber, finely
sliced into strips

20 coriander leaves

GADO-GADO DRESSING

75 g smooth peanut
butter

1 tablespoon sweet
chilli sauce

2 tablespoons dark
soy sauce

MAKES 20

Crisp salad leaves, such as chicory (Belgian endive or witloof) and Little Gem, make wonderful edible scoops. Filled with a classic Indonesian salad, these leaf cups are a refreshing and colourful addition to any party menu. Quails' eggs could have been specially invented for finger food, although they can be difficult to peel. If you can't find them, top the salad with finely chopped hard-boiled egg instead.

gado-gado salad

in chicory leaves

To make the dressing, put the peanut butter in a bowl, add 2 tablespoons boiling water and, using a fork, mix quickly until the mixture is completely smooth. Stir in the chilli sauce and soy sauce.

Put the quails' eggs in a small saucepan of cold water and bring to the boil. Simmer for 3 minutes, then drain immediately and cool under cold running water. Peel, then cut into quarters.

Trim the chicory and separate into 20 leaves. To assemble, fill the leaves with the bean sprouts and strips of each vegetable. Using a teaspoon, drizzle the gado-gado sauce over the top, then add the coriander leaves and quails' egg quarters and serve.

NOTE: If you are catering for large numbers, it may be easier and quicker to pipe the dressing over the salad. Use a piping bag fitted with a 3 mm plain nozzle or plastic sandwich bag with the tip of a corner snipped off.

vegetarian sushi roll

Making sushi might require skill and practice, but simple rolled sushi is very straightforward. This vegetarian version (minus the raw fish) is a stunning canapé, first course or even a meal in itself. It's important to use sushi rice, which cooks to the right sticky consistency. Serve with traditional Japanese accompaniments: sweet, pink pickled ginger and a little dish of soy sauce for dipping. Don't forget the hot wasabi paste, but warn people that

only a tiny amount is needed for that fiery horseradish sensation.

250 ml sushi rice, measured by volume

2–3 tablespoons Japanese rice vinegar or sushi vinegar

a pinch of salt

1 tablespoon mirin (Japanese sweet rice wine) (optional)

3–4 sheets nori seaweed

¼ firm ripe avocado, halved, pitted and cut lengthways into thin strips and brushed lightly with lemon juice

10 cm cucumber, deseeded and cut into long thin strips

½ red pepper, deseeded and cut lengthways into thin strips

toasted sesame seeds

TO SERVE

Japanese soy sauce

wasabi paste (hot green horseradish)

pink pickled ginger

a sushi rolling mat or heavy-duty foil

MAKES 20–30 PIECES

1 Put the rice in a sieve and wash well under cold running water until the water is clear. Drain, let stand for at least 30 minutes, then transfer to a heavy-based saucepan.

2 Pour in enough water to cover the rice by 2 cm. Cover with a lid and bring to the boil, then reduce the heat and simmer for about 15 minutes until the water is absorbed. Remove the lid, cover the pan with a clean tea towel and replace the lid. Let rest for 10 minutes.

3 Transfer the cooked rice to a large non-metal bowl. (A brown skin may have formed around the pan: simply scrape the rice away from it.) Add the vinegar, salt and mirin, if using, and mix. For perfect sticky rice, stand the bowl near an electric fan, stirring the rice until cooled.

4 To make the sushi rolls, toast the nori over a very low gas flame or electric hotplate for a few seconds until crisp, then put, shiny side down, on the mat or foil. Using wet fingers, put a handful of rice in the centre of the nori and spread it over the top, leaving a 2 cm band uncovered nearest to you. Using the back of your finger, press a shallow groove down the middle of the rice.

5 Lay 1–2 strips of the avocado, cucumber and pepper in the groove (do not overfill or you will have difficulty rolling up the sushi). Lightly sprinkle with the toasted sesame seeds.

6 Roll the mat or foil, starting from the front edge and rolling away from you, so that the rice and filling are enclosed in the nori. Dampen the edge of the nori if it doesn't stick once rolled. Remove the rolled sushi and put, join side down, in a flat container while you make the remaining rolls in the same way.

7 Using a sharp knife dipped in hot water, trim and discard the ends, then cut the roll into 1 cm thick pieces. Serve with soy sauce, pink pickled ginger and wasabi. The sushi can be made several hours in advance, left whole, wrapped in clingfilm and left in a cool place until needed, but do eat on the day of making.

chocolate banana cheesecake

Chocolate and banana are natural partners in this luxuriously wicked cheesecake. Mascarpone makes the pudding lighter by reducing the cloying texture of the cream cheese.

BISCUIT BASE

200 g plain chocolate-covered digestive biscuits

50 g unsalted butter, melted

2 tablespoons cocoa powder

CHEESECAKE FILLING

400 g cream cheese or curd cheese

250 g mascarpone cheese

2 large ripe bananas, broken into chunks

2 teaspoons pure vanilla extract

200 g caster sugar

2 eggs, lightly beaten

TOPPING

100 g plain chocolate, chopped

50 g unsalted butter, cut into cubes

1 large banana

juice of ½ lemon

24 cm springform cake tin, greased

SERVES 8–10

Crush the biscuits in a food processor, then transfer to a bowl. Pour in the melted butter, add the cocoa and mix well. Tip the crumbs into the prepared tin and press firmly with the back of a spoon or your fingertips. Bake in a preheated oven at 180°C (350°F) Gas 4 for about 10 minutes. Let cool. Reduce the oven temperature to 150°C (300°F) Gas 2.

To make the filling, put the cheeses in a food processor and blend until smooth. Add the bananas, vanilla and sugar and mix well. Add the eggs, a little at a time, and pulse until smooth. Alternatively, beat the ingredients, as above, in a bowl until smooth. Pour into the tin and bake for 30–40 minutes, until just set but still slightly wobbly in the middle (it will set firmer as it cools). Let cool in the tin, then chill for at least 3 hours or overnight.

To make the topping, melt the chocolate and butter in a heatproof bowl set over a saucepan of simmering water.

Unmould the cheesecake, but don't remove the bottom of the tin – the biscuit base may break. Transfer to a serving plate. Top with the chocolate mixture and spread, letting it dribble over the edge. Cut the banana diagonally into long slices, toss in the lemon juice to prevent the pieces discolouring, pat dry, then arrange in a circle on top of the cheesecake. Chill until the topping is set. Serve.

sweet things

carrot and olive oil cake

Fruity olive oil makes this carrot cake like no other. Deliciously moist and lightly spiced, it's this type of cake that is helping to revitalize vegetarian food. It's gorgeous – and couldn't be easier to make: you don't even need a mixer.

250 ml olive oil

500 g caster sugar

4 eggs, beaten

250 g plain flour

2 teaspoons baking powder

2 teaspoons bicarbonate of soda

2 teaspoons ground cinnamon

1 teaspoon ground cloves

1 teaspoon ground cardamom (optional)

1 teaspoon sea salt

125 g pecans or walnuts, coarsely chopped

500 g carrots, peeled and grated

MASCARPONE ICING

125 g unsalted butter, softened

2 teaspoons pure vanilla extract

250 g mascarpone cheese or cream cheese

250 g icing sugar

24 cm springform cake tin, base-lined with baking parchment, greased and lightly dusted with flour

SERVES 8–10

Put the olive oil, sugar and eggs in a bowl and stir until well mixed. Sift the flour and other dry ingredients into a second bowl and make a well in the centre. Add the egg and oil mixture and mix thoroughly until blended. Add the pecan or walnuts and carrots and mix well.

Pour into the prepared cake tin and bake in a preheated oven at 170°C (325°F) Gas 3 for 1 hour 20 minutes, until a skewer inserted into the centre comes out clean. Let cool in the tin, then run a knife around the edge of the cake to loosen and turn out.

To make the icing, mix the butter, vanilla and mascarpone or cream cheese in a food processor or bowl. Gradually add the icing sugar and mix until smooth and creamy. Do not overmix or the icing may curdle. Spread onto the cake and make patterns in the top.

white chocolate mousse torte

This no-bake pudding is not for the faint-hearted. You will only be able to manage a slender slice, but, believe me, it's all you need. I've had varying results with this recipe. Sometimes the texture is mousse-like, other times like truffles, but it's always divine. Serve after dinner with strong black coffee.

BISCUIT BASE

200 g amaretti biscuits

100 g unsalted butter, melted

MOUSSE

350 g white chocolate

500 ml double cream, at room temperature

4 tablespoons milk, at room temperature

24 cm springform cake tin, greased and lined with a collar of baking parchment

SERVES 12

Crush the amaretti biscuits in a food processor until they look like fine crumbs, then transfer to a bowl and mix in the melted butter. Tip the mixture into the prepared cake tin and press firmly over the base with the back of a spoon or your fingertips.

Break the chocolate into pieces and melt in a heatproof bowl set over a saucepan of simmering water. Set aside and let cool until lukewarm.

Put the cream and milk in a bowl and, using an electric hand-held mixer, whisk until the mixture leaves a ribbon-like trail on the surface when the mixer is lifted out of the bowl.

Using a large metal spoon, stir a spoonful of the whipped cream mixture into the chocolate to slacken, then immediately pour it into the remaining cream mixture. Stir vigorously until smooth and mousse-like. Don't worry if there are tiny lumps of chocolate flecked in the mixture – it will still taste delicious.

Pour into the prepared tin and swirl the top. Cover and refrigerate for at least 4 hours or overnight. When set, remove the tin, but leave the base on and peel off the paper collar. Let stand for a few minutes to soften, then cut into thin slices and serve.

raspberry roulade

Pure indulgence is a crisp meringue with a soft, marshmallow centre, filled with whipped cream and topped with berries. Once mastered, you'll discover that a meringue is one of the simplest, prettiest and most versatile of all puddings. You can use the basic recipe to make individual shells, then fill with lemon curd, cream and seasonal fruit. Shells bake in a cool oven at 120°C (250°F) Gas ½ for 45 minutes. Here I've used the meringue to make a feather-light roulade, which cooks in just 17 minutes. Sharp-flavoured fruits, such as raspberries, balance the sweetness of the meringue, though you could use any of your favourite fruits – it's up to you.

MERINGUE

6 egg whites, at room temperature

a pinch of sea salt

375 g caster sugar

2 teaspoons cornflour

1 teaspoon white wine vinegar

RASPBERRY ROSE FILLING

500 ml double cream

3–6 tablespoons rose water

250 g raspberries

a 30 x 40 cm shallow cake tin lined with baking parchment

SERVES 8–10

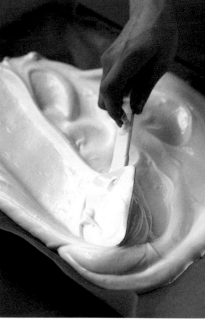

1 Put the egg whites and salt in a scrupulously clean, dry bowl and, using an electric hand-held mixer, whisk until stiff peaks form. (Take care: if there is any trace of egg yolk or moisture in the bowl the whites won't whisk properly.)

2 Sprinkle in 1 tablespoon of sugar at a time and whisk between each addition until the meringue is thick and glossy. Add the cornflour and vinegar and whisk until mixed.

3 Transfer to the prepared baking tin and, using a spatula, spread the meringue into the corners of the tin and smooth the surface. Bake in a preheated oven at 180°C (350°F) Gas 4 for 17 minutes or until barely crisp. Let cool.

4 To turn out the meringue, cover with a sheet of parchment paper, then quickly but carefully invert the tin onto the work surface. Lift off the tin, then gently peel off the lining paper from the meringue.

5 To make the filling, put the cream and rose water in a bowl and whip lightly until softly peaking. Spoon onto the meringue and spread, leaving a 1 cm border clear all round. Add the raspberries.

6 Lift up the side of the baking parchment nearest to you and use it to help roll up the roulade lengthways. Peel back the paper as you go. Before you reach the end, carefully lift the roulade (still on the paper) onto a platter or board.

7 Roll the roulade off the paper so that the join is underneath, then slice into 8–10 pieces and serve.

champagne jelly

100 g blueberries

100 g small seedless red grapes

500 ml champagne or sparkling wine

50 g caster sugar

3 teaspoons vegetarian gelatin (agar agar)

SERVES 4

Divide the blueberries and red grapes between 4 tall glasses or champagne flutes. Pour half the champagne or sparkling wine into a saucepan and add the sugar and gelatin. Heat gently, stirring until the sugar and gelatin have dissolved, then heat until almost boiling.

Slowly add the remaining fizz. Pour into the glasses and chill for 3 hours or until softly set. Serve immediately – the jelly will soften the longer it is out of the refrigerator.

jellies

Bright jellies wobbling on a plate are a childhood favourite, but here are two delicious grown-up versions that you just have to try. Gelatin, though it may look and taste innocent, is not suitable for vegetarians. Luckily, there is an alternative derived from seaweed, which can now be found in most supermarkets, as well as health food stores.

thai coconut jelly

Put the milk, lemongrass, lime leaves, ginger and chilli in a saucepan, bring to the boil and simmer for 15 minutes. Remove from the heat and let cool.

Strain the infused milk into a jug and add enough coconut milk to make up to 500 ml. Discard the flavourings and reserve the remaining coconut milk for another use. Return the infused milk to the pan and, using an electric hand-held mixer, whisk in the sugar and gelatin until dissolved. Heat gently, whisking continuously, until almost boiling, then transfer to a jug (for easy pouring).

Pour into 4 glass bowls. Let cool, then chill for 3 hours or until set. To serve, sprinkle with chopped peanuts.

250 ml milk

2 stalks lemongrass, sliced

2 kaffir lime leaves, coarsely chopped

2 cm fresh ginger, unpeeled and sliced

1 small red chilli, cut in half

1 can coconut milk, about 400 ml

125 g caster sugar

3 teaspoons vegetarian gelatin (agar agar)

honey-roasted peanuts, chopped, to serve

SERVES 4

An elegant pudding that can be made well ahead of time. For a special occasion, it's nice to stuff the pears, but, if the long list of ingredients and preparation put you off, then just omit this part. Simply serve the poached pears whole with the luscious syrup spooned over.

mulled wine pears

with spiced stuffing

4 firm, ripe pears

1 vanilla pod, split in half lengthways

250 ml freshly squeezed orange juice

500 ml red wine

125 g sugar

grated zest of 2 lemons

6 whole cloves

1 cinnamon stick

crème fraîche, to serve

SPICED STUFFING

75 g hazelnuts

1 tablespoon soft brown sugar

2 tablespoons currants or sultanas

1 teaspoon ground cinnamon

¼ teaspoon ground cloves

a large pinch of freshly grated nutmeg

1½ tablespoons orange flower water

a large pinch of sea salt

SERVES 4

Peel the pears, leaving the stems intact. Cut a thin slice off the bottom of each one, so they stand upright, and scoop out the cores with a teaspoon. Scrape the seeds from the vanilla pod into a large saucepan, then add the pod and the orange juice, red wine, sugar, lemon zest, cloves and cinnamon. Bring to the boil, stirring until the sugar has dissolved. Gently lower the pears on their side into the pan and simmer, turning frequently in the poaching liquid, for 30 minutes, until tender (depending on ripeness).

Using a slotted spoon, remove the pears from the poaching liquid and set aside to cool. Strain the liquid and return to the pan. Heat until reduced and syrupy. Let cool.

To make the stuffing, roast the hazelnuts in a preheated oven at 200°C (400°F) Gas 6 for 5 minutes, until lightly golden. Let cool. Put in a food processor, whizz until ground, then add the remaining ingredients and pulse until mixed. Spoon the mixture into the hollowed-out poached pears and spread a thin layer on the bottom of each one (this will help the pears stand upright when you put them on the plates). Serve with the syrup poured over and a dollop of crème fraîche.

200 g unsalted butter

200 g demerara sugar

200 g honey

400 g porridge oats

50 g nuts, dried fruits or
glacé ginger, chopped
or desiccated coconut
(optional)

a 20 x 30 cm shallow
cake tin, greased

MAKES 12

Put the butter, sugar and honey in
a saucepan and heat, stirring
occasionally, until the butter has melted
and the sugar has dissolved. Add the
oats and nuts, fruit, ginger or coconut,
if using, and mix well.

Transfer the oat mixture to the prepared
cake tin and spread to about 2 cm
thick. Smooth the surface with the
back of a spoon. Bake in a preheated
oven at 180°C (350°F) Gas 4 for
15–20 minutes, until lightly golden
around the edges, but still slightly soft
in the middle. Let cool in the tin, then
turn out and cut into squares.

honey flapjacks

These wonderful chewy oat bars are
practically effortless to make. You don't have
to be an expert baker to have a go. Flapjacks
are perfect teatime treats or mid-morning
snacks. They also travel well – wrap for
a picnic or packed lunch.

chocolate chunk nut cookies

Simple to make, absolutely divine taste, crisp on the outside, soft and gooey in the middle – what more could you ask for? Vary the nuts to suit yourself: I'm fond of pecans, macadamias and pine nuts, but you can use walnuts or hazelnuts. Keep the chocolate and nuts chunky for maximum impact.

125 g plain flour

½ teaspoon baking powder

½ teaspoon sea salt

125 g unsalted butter, softened

100 g soft brown sugar

1 teaspoon pure vanilla essence

1 egg

200 g plain chocolate (70 per cent cocoa solids), coarsely chopped

50 g nuts, such as pecans or hazelnuts, coarsely chopped

a large baking sheet, lined with baking parchment

MAKES 12–14

Put all the ingredients, except the chocolate and nuts, in a food processor and whizz until mixed. Stir in the chocolate and nuts. Alternatively, sift the flour, baking powder and salt into a bowl. Put the butter, sugar and vanilla in another bowl and beat with a wooden spoon or electric mixer, until light and fluffy. Gradually beat in the egg. Fold in the flour mixture. Mix in the chocolate and nuts.

Scrape the cookie dough onto a large square of clingfilm and roll into a 30 cm long sausage shape. Twist the ends to seal and chill for at least 30 minutes or until firm.

When ready to bake, unwrap the dough and cut into 2 cm thick slices. Put 3 cm apart on the prepared baking sheet (in batches, if necessary) and bake in a preheated oven at 190°C (375°F) Gas 5 for 15–20 minutes, until just golden. Transfer to a wire rack and let cool.

menu ideas

JAPANESE LUNCH
Vegetarian sushi roll

Japanese omelette

Char-grilled asparagus and leaf salad with sesame-soy dressing

THAI SUPPER
Thai coleslaw

Pad Thai noodles

Thai coconut jelly

LIGHT MIDDLE EASTERN LUNCH
Baba ganouj with warm flatbread

Warm chickpea salad with spiced mushrooms

A FEAST FOR THE EYES
(a particularly beautiful but not too complicated meal)

Pumpkin and tofu laksa

Raspberry roulade

SUMMER SALAD FEAST
Saffron potato salad

Tuscan panzanella

Minted char-grilled courgettes

Green salad with blue cheese dressing I

MEXICAN INDIAN SUMMER SUPPER
Mexican gazpacho

Haloumi fajitas

Chocolate banana cheesecake

MEXICAN ALL-YEAR SUPPER OR LUNCH
Quesadillas

Tamales

Chocolate banana cheesecake

WARMING WINTER DINNER
Shiitake and field mushroom soup with Madeira and thyme

Braised chicory and beans with smoked cheese mash

Raspberry roulade

DEEP-HEAT WINTER LUNCH
Lemon-potato latkes with gingered avocado crème

Charred aubergine and coconut curry

Carrot and olive oil cake

SIMPLE WINTER LUNCH
Caramelized onion and Gruyère focaccia

Lentil, coconut and wilted spinach soup

ITALIAN DINNER WITH POLENTA IN TWO GUISES
Stuffed polenta mushrooms

Piedmontese peppers with gorgonzola polenta

VEGETARIAN CHRISTMAS I
Celeriac, saffron and orange soup

Chestnut, spinach and mushroom filo torte with red ginger coulis

Lemon-roasted baby potatoes

Greens with pine nuts and redcurrants (see Chilli greens with crispy garlic)

Mulled wine pears with spiced stuffing

VEGETARIAN CHRISTMAS II
Topped bruschetta with wild mushrooms with apples and Madeira

Torta di risotto with three cheeses

Chilli greens with crispy garlic

Roasted sweet potatoes with shallots, garlic and chilli

White chocolate mousse torte

CHRISTMAS DRINKS PARTY
Mushroom and onion marmalade tartlets

Spinach and water chestnut wontons

Mini lemon potato latkes with gingered avocado crème

Spiced roasted nuts

Stuffed polenta mushrooms

SUMMER DRINKS PARTY
Vegetarian sushi roll

Mozzarella and cherry tomato skewers

Feta and cumin filo parcels

Crudités with sesame yoghurt dip

Topped bruschetta with slow-roasted tomatoes

BARBECUE I
Parmesan patties

Feta stuffed peppers

Thai-glazed vegetable skewers

Caesar salad

BARBECUE II
Turkish stuffed aubergines

Stuffed flat mushrooms with mozzarella and truffle oil

Thai-glazed vegetable skewers

Char-grilled asparagus and leaf salad with sesame-soy dressing

A LUNCH OF SMALL COURSES
Baba ganouj and sesame yoghurt dip with warm flatbread

Topped bruschetta with wild mushrooms with apples and Madeira

Piedmontese peppers

Champagne jelly

FUSS-FREE AUTUMN DINNER
Shiitake and field mushroom soup with Madeira and thyme

Vegetarian sausages and mash with thyme and mushroom gravy

Provençal roasted vegetables

Raspberry roulade

FULL-ON BRUNCH BUFFET FOR 14
Cottage cheese pancakes

Japanese omelette with grilled tomatoes and avocado

Breakfast burritos

Corn muffins

Caesar salad

Honey flapjacks

Chocolate chunk nut cookies

index